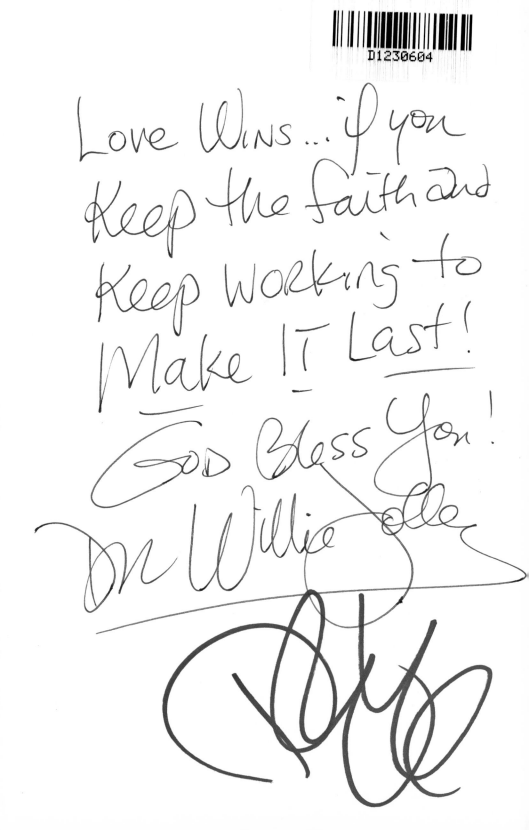

Love Wins... if you
Keep the faith and
Keep Working to
Make IT Last!
God Bless You!
Dr. Willie Jolley

From the Bestselling author of
A Setback Is A Setup For A Comeback!

Make LOVE,

Make MONEY,

Make IT LAST!

10 SECRETS TO SHAPE A GREAT MARRIAGE!

Written by
(Best Selling Author and Hall of Fame Speaker)
Dr. Willie Jolley
and (his bride of over 30 years)
Dee Taylor-Jolley, M. Ed.

OTHER BOOKS BY
DR. WILLIE JOLLEY

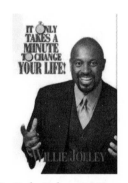

It Only Takes A Minute
To Change Your Life!

A Setback Is A Setup
For A Comeback

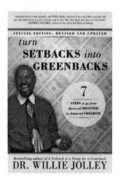

Turn Setbacks Into
Greenbacks

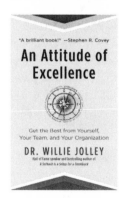

Get the Best from
Yourself, Your
Team and Your
Organization

ISBN: Print Book - 978-0-9815074-0-8

Book design by: Jessica Angerstein

Photography by: Ron Baker

PROUDLY PRINTED IN
THE UNITED STATES OF AMERICA
By Jolley Life Publishing

SPECIAL SALES
Willie Jolley Books are available at a
special discount for bulk purchases for
sales promotions and premiums.
For more details email: info@williejolley.com
Or call (202) 723-8863

This book is dedicated to our parents,
Rev. Rivers S. Taylor, Sr. and First Lady, Lillie Mae Taylor
and Levi H. Jolley and Catherine B. Jolley for their
wonderful examples of marriage for us to model.

Contents

Gratitude & Acknowledgments 1

Foreword 5

Let's Start with Why 7

Introduction 11

Chapter 1   Friends First. 17

Chapter 2   Make God an Equal Part in Your Marriage 29

Chapter 3   Decide to Make It Last 41

Chapter 4   Communicate! Talk to Each Other 57

Chapter 5   Leave the Drama with Your Mama! 79

Chapter 6   Agree about Disagreeing 91

Chapter 7   How to Handle a Stalemate 99

Chapter 8   Sex, Headaches, and Other Lies 113

Chapter 9   Always Date Your Mate 131

Chapter 10   Count the Costs: Money Matters 143

*Special Section – Message For Singles:
How To Choose The Right Person To Marry! 157

Lyrics from "Little Things" 169

Final Thoughts 173

Gratitude & Acknowledgments

Moving dining room chairs back to the table, sweeping up food crumbs from the family room floor, and bundling up garbage was really challenging at 12:30 in the morning after the anniversary celebration our son had for us. Our son, William, had given us a 30th wedding anniversary celebration (at our home), telling us he was inviting "a few friends" to "celebrate" our marriage. The few friends turned out to be over 100 people, (some we didn't know) and the "celebration" turned out to be us sharing our marriage secrets with this huge gathering of millennials.

"Mom and Dad, everyone asks me all the time about you two and how much they enjoy spending time with you because you seem to be so in love. Please tell them how you guys make it work," William said. The "it" is our marriage. So, we all ate pizza as we shared our ideas on developing a successful relationship. The idea for this book was solidified then.

We started talking about writing a book and each time we mentioned it we got the same response, "Yes! Please! Please! Please! Write what you have shared with us over the years!" We thought the title of the book would be "Jolley Tips For Marriage" then Delatorro McNeal came to visit and gave us a startling revelation. Delatorro is one of the top young speakers in America and one of our "adopted" children. We helped him get started in the speaking industry and he typically stays with us when he comes to DC. Over dinner, we told him about the book and he said, "Praise the Lord! Finally, you two are going to do what I have been praying for, sharing your marriage and relationship secrets in a book!" He went on to tell us that everywhere he goes people ask about us and want to know how we have created our successful business and marriage, and seem to enjoy the journey. Delatorro then gave us the title that he had been thinking about, if we ever decided to write our marriage book…"*Make Love, Make Money, Make It Last!*" We loved it!!!!

So, we start our book with gratitude for all who have helped to make it a reality. We are grateful for our children, William and Sherry, who openly and lovingly shared their stories. Grateful for our "adopted" children, Delatorro McNeal II, for his great ideas and encouragement and Cheryl Ragin, for helping to manage our office and our lives. Grateful to Dr. Ro for her foreword and for her encouragement and friendship. Grateful to book publishing expert, David Wildasin for all his wise counsel. Grateful to Nina Taylor for her great editing services. Grateful to Bill and Vivian Clark for their input and ideas after 40 years of marriage and for their willingness to read our drafts and to continue to love us in spite of us always sending them updates to read.

In this book, we share the principles we have used to create a joy-filled and loving marriage, but we also share tips and strategies we have learned from other happily married couples. While we've been positively impacted by countless examples of successful marriages, here are a few people we'd like to give special thanks to for sharing their ideas that have led to their healthy, happy, vibrant marriages.

GRATITUDE AND ACKNOWLEDGEMENTS

- ♥ Kenneth and Bernice Mitchell, married over 60 years.

- ♥ Jim and Naomi Rhode, married and in business together for more than 60 years.

- ♥ Herman and Claudia Thompson, married over 50 years.

- ♥ Dr. Clarice Fluitt, author, minister, professional speaker, married over 50 years.

- ♥ Sanford and Linda Berman, married for over 50 years.

- ♥ Jerry and Isabel Jasinowski, married over 40 years.

- ♥ Kenny and Rudene Glass, married over 40 years.

- ♥ Dayal and Varkha Alwani of St Maarten, married over 40 years.

- ♥ Al and Tee Way, married for over 35 years.

- ♥ Pastor John K. Jenkins, Sr. and First Lady Trina Jenkins, married for over 35 years.

- ♥ Ron and Gladys Pemberton, married over 35 years.

- ♥ Jeffrey and Denise Hart, married over 35 years.

- ♥ Bradley and Terry Thomas, married over 30 years.

- ♥ John and Kathy Morgan, married over 30 years.

- ♥ Ronny and Olenthia Boardley, married over 25 years.

- ♥ Rhonda and Tim Smith, married for over 25 years.

- ♥ B Smith and Dan Gasby, married and in business together over 20 years.

- ♥ Adam and Marissa Levin, married and in business together over 20 years.

- ♥ Rivers and Shirley Taylor, married over 25 years.

- ♥ Stephen and Andi Bullock, married later in life.

Other major contributors:

Bishop A.J. Wright

Michelle Singletary, Washington Post Syndicated Financial Columnist

Zemira Jones, media consultant

Jane Herlong, humorist, professional speaker, author

Kevin Toney, author, Breaking the Men's Code

John Stoddart, song writer, "You Are"
(his wife Helen is his inspiration)

Foreword
DR. RO

Most people across America know me as Dr. Ro, America's nutrition coach, media personality and best-selling author. Most people do not know that I grew up in inner city Washington DC and after my mother died, I transferred to Roosevelt Senior High School, where I met Willie and Dee.

I have known Willie and Dee since I was 16 years old. We have grown together, traveled together, laughed together and cried together. The truth is we've been together so long that we're no longer just friends, we're family.

When I have a major book tour, I always opt to stay with them when the tour comes to Washington, DC rather than staying at a hotel. Their home is filled with love and lots of great life lessons. During a recent press tour for my latest book, *Lose Your Final 15,* I stayed at their house for 2 full weeks. Although I had known them for decades, living with them presented a rare opportunity to see their unique expressions of love up close and personal.

I observed that Willie makes Dee feel like the only woman on earth when he's in her presence. And when Willie enters the room, Dee makes him feel like the most important person on the planet regardless of what's happening, whether it happens to be an intense business discussion or any other matters, there is nothing of greater importance to her at the time than her Willie. That takes a special kind of dedication, thoughtfulness, and mindfulness that I've never seen demonstrated by any other couple. That they've jointly managed a marriage and a business for over three decades is impressive. That they've done so without having an argument is a miracle! Yet they share often, that was not always the case. The principles they learned through their challenges, have allowed them to stop arguing and start loving!

I have learned more about how to maintain a happy and healthy marriage from these two than I have from anyone. As a friend and mentor, Dee has shared the kind of wisdom and sage advice over the years that has made me a better wife. Plus I learned how to be a better business partner with my husband. I couldn't pay for the lessons, nor the blessings I have received from Dee and Willie.

The information you'll receive in the pages that follow, will not only bless you as it has blessed me and my husband, but if you heed their advice, you'll find a grounded level of peace, happiness, and love in your own relationship. They walk the talk that they teach in this book…read it and use it as a guide and I am confident you will be very happy with the results.

In Love, Health, and Happiness
xox

Dr. Ro
Dr. Rovenia Brock

Let's Start with Why

Dee and I wrote this book to help couples create great married lives. We want couples to enjoy the state of being married just as much as we do. If you want more fun and less drama, more sweet talk and less arguing, more romance and less distance, then this book is for you. We want you to make love, make money, and make it last!

Often, we are asked by those who've met our son, William, "Is it true what he's told us—that you have not had an argument in over thirty years?" "Yes, it's true," we tell them. Plus, we're together about twenty hours a day! We work together, travel together, play together, and pray together! We've learned how to stay happily married, and we are excited to share what we've learned and what works for us. We believe it will work for you as well.

While at a dinner party, a friend mentioned he had heard me on my SiriusXM Radio show talking about tips from our new marriage book, and he was really intrigued by the ten points I shared. While he was talking, our conversation was interrupted by a lady who was standing next to us. She said she was having marital issues herself and wanted to know more about the concepts we discussed in our book. When I told her that the main points were listed on the pre-release information on my website, she was not satisfied. She begged me to share the points. She said she was desperate and needed that information right then. So I gave her the "Reader's Digest" version of the book.

You might be in a similar place, where you need the main points immediately. Or you might be getting ready to get married and want advice right now, before you say I do!

Here are the ten points we recommend:

1. **Friends first.** Be or become friends, because it's hard to have long-lasting love or a long-lasting marriage with someone you don't really like.

2. **Make God an equal part of your marriage.** In fact, make Him the majority part of the marriage.

3. **Decide to make it last!** Love is an emotion, but marriage is a decision.

4. **Communicate! Talk to each other.** Your mate is not a mind reader.

5. **Leave the drama with your mama!** Never stir up emotions to create confusion.

6. **Agree on how you will disagree** before challenging situations arise.

7. **Learn how to manage a stalemate.** Decide on your strategy to break a tie before you need it!

8. **Sex, headaches, and other lies:** the truth about sex versus intimacy.

9. **Always date your mate.**

10. **Count the costs! Money matters.** Marriage is not just a love relationship, it is a business relationship as well.

The question has been asked, who is this book for? It is for anyone presently in a relationship—currently married, dating —as well as those looking to get into a successful relationship that leads to marriage. If you are presently married and doing fine, then you will enjoy the stories, ideas, and principles presented in this book. If you are married and having some challenges or serious problems, you NEED to read this book and practice our advice. And finally, if you are single and interested in finding the right person to marry, you MUST read this book before you make any decisions. This book is written with a goal of informing, instructing, inspiring, and empowering people to have better relationships, and to enjoy the marriage journey with more commitment and excitement.

We believe your home should be your castle and sanctuary, where the husband and wife make up the royal family. This is a place where the husband is treated like the king of the castle and the wife is treated like a queen and placed on a pedestal.

Unfortunately, far too often we hear stories where the home is a war zone, and the enemies are the married people who live within the house! They get so caught up in winning their individual skirmishes that they lose the bigger prize of a happily married relationship. If you want your home to be your castle and not a war zone, keep reading.

Introduction

"What I like most about my home ...
is who I share it with!"
~ Tad Carpenter

DR. WILLIE JOLLEY'S PERSPECTIVE

I am Dr. Willie Jolley, and I am married to the beautiful and brilliant Dee Taylor-Jolley. We've been married for over thirty years, and have raised two children. We are a blended family; our oldest child was ten years of age when we married. Our youngest was born of this union. We write this book having gone through many of the same challenges you may be presently going through, have gone through, or you might go through!

This book is the result of our children and their friends pushing and prodding us to write what we share with them about life, relationships, and successful marriages. Over the years, we've shared our insights with dating couples, married couples, and those preparing to be married. We've listened and asked the tough questions; prayed and prodded couples to work through their challenges; and provided advice on building positive, healthy relationships and marriages.

The needs of the couples have varied widely. Some were working on how to communicate their wants, needs, and hurts more effectively. Some wanted to create a "drama-free" culture at home. Some were desperately working on fixing their broken marriages. And many just wanted to know how to begin their marriages so that their love, excitement, and respect would last!

While we've been married for over three decades, we still act like newlyweds. It is not by chance or happenstance that we still act this way. We have learned how to live happily and peacefully together and have taught others to do the same. Whenever we share that we have not had an argument in over thirty years, the questions start to fly. How? How do you do this? Eventually, we realized we needed a tool that people could study to build better relationships and marriages for themselves.

The final push to write this book came from a friend who was in a business meeting I was attending. During the meeting, she acknowledged she could not focus on the business issues being discussed because her marriage was falling apart. She was angry at her husband because she felt he was no longer the man she had married twenty years earlier.

For the next hour of the meeting, she complained about her marriage and her husband. She was trying to figure out how to leave him without destroying her children emotionally. She lamented that she was a child of divorce and remembered the negative impact divorce had on her and her siblings. While she did not want the same for her children, she saw little hope of a better way.

After an hour of listening to her tearful comments, I told her I would be happy to talk to her husband. She felt their marriage was beyond repair, but for the sake of the kids, she was willing to give it one last try.

I had dinner with her husband several days later and shared the principles Dee and I have used to stay happily married. I told him that these were not just principles that have worked for us, but also for numerous couples we have counseled. He listened. He did not say much. I wasn't sure he'd gotten the concepts, but as we ended our time together, he shook my hand and with tears in his eyes, thanked me. He said, "No one had ever shared ideas like these with me." The only ideas he had ever been exposed to about marriage were either from his divorced parents, or friends who were also struggling in their own marriages.

After the dinner meeting, I called his wife and told her the exact same things I shared with him and explained what she needed to work on as well. They both had work to do if this was to succeed. She listened. She agreed to work on it and would wait to see if he would do the same.

I got a call from the wife a few weeks later, exclaiming she had a changed husband! He was not the same man. Her children even noticed and had asked, "Is Dad on medication?" A few weeks later, she called again and said her life had changed drastically, and that she was so happy, she really didn't know what to do. She said that she had been telling everyone that Willie Jolley is "not only a great motivational speaker, but is really the marriage whisperer!" I had to laugh, but I was mostly grateful that I had been able to share some principles that helped.

"Will you please share your ideas in a book," she asked? "It would be a blessing to so many who are struggling with relationships and hurting and desperate for help with broken and painful marriages. I know you are busy, but please make time to do this, because it saved my marriage and it could save a lot more!"

That was it. Her plea was the final straw. We went to work on this book. I told Dee we had to help others, not just the people we personally counsel, but people everywhere, whenever they needed it. Out of that desire, the writing of this book became a priority!

DEE TAYLOR-JOLLEY'S PERSPECTIVE

Although it's difficult for me to share my innermost thoughts publicly, I decided to write this book with my husband because he convinced me to tell my story, warts and all because it would help others. The challenge is, I have a secret!

My son, William, said, "Mom, my friends say you changed their lives. They came to visit to talk to Dad, but once they spoke with you and you shared your advice and insights, they were mesmerized. You need to share your thoughts in a book." I appreciated William sharing this information with me, but people don't know that I have a secret!

I met a young lady at a church where Willie was the guest speaker. She shared how impressed she was with how Willie spoke so glowingly of me and our relationship during his message. She confided that she would love to have her husband speak of her in a similar way. Then she shared they were having major marriage problems. She was in a women's support group with others who were struggling in their marriages, and she wanted me to speak to them. As the tears welled up in her eyes, I realized I could help, but my secret made me reluctant to accept her offer.

What is my secret? My secret is that I am extremely introverted. I appreciate quiet time, reading good books, and intimate one-on-one conversations with family and friends.

How can an introvert remain successfully married to a motivational speaker, who shares everything with the world on a daily basis? It's simple, but not easy: I put on my "extroverted armor" and force myself to do what I find most uncomfortable.

By agreeing to this project, I also agreed to remove myself from my protective shield and expose my heart and philosophy on marriage success. To be successful in marriage and being a partner in business is hard work. I think of myself like the duck who appears to glide effortlessly across a pond—if you look beneath the surface, its webbed feet are working really hard!

My persuasive husband and son convinced me that my perspective, my view of life, and my blunt honesty would have value for an audience beyond my kitchen table. That is the motivation and hope that got me to share my thoughts in this book. So…here I am!

CHAPTER ONE

Friends First!

(BE OR BECOME FRIENDS FIRST)

*"It is not a lack of love,
but a lack of friendship
that makes unhappy marriages."*
~ Friedrich Nietzsche

WILLIE'S PERSPECTIVE

It's hard to have a long-lasting, loving marriage with someone you don't really like.

We are in a time of social media, where you connect with people online who are called friends, but you really don't know them, i.e. "Facebook friends." Yet, when we speak of a friend in this book, we are talking about something different than a social media friend.

We believe a friend is a person you know well and who knows you well. The two of you have mutual affection and trust. They stand by you in good times and bad times, happy times and sad times. A true friend will stand with you, stand by you, and stand up for you. This is someone you can depend on to have your back.

A study by the National Bureau of Economic Research in Canada, released in December 2014, found that if you want to be happily married, you need to make a point that the person you marry is your best friend. In the study, happiness was measured using three groups: 1) newlyweds; 2) those after the honeymoon phase, who were married for a few years, and able to maintain their happiness; and 3) folks who were able to maintain their marriage and happiness during their middle age years, especially after their children had left the home.

Studies show that not only are people physically different at middle age, but they are emotionally different. The research reveals that those who are married to their best friend tend to handle the changes dramatically better. All three groups had higher levels of happiness than their counterparts when they were married to their best friends. They had twice as much happiness and life satisfaction from their marriages. It's in those marriages that the spouses were able to help each other through the tough times. They were willing to work together, struggle together, grow together, and stay together.

Dee and I can attest to the fact that our marriage has flourished because we were good friends before we got married. Over the years, our friendship has grown and matured, and we are not only good friends, but best friends. But this does not mean that we were just two friends who decided to get married! I thought Dee was beautiful when we started dating and still think so today, but her beauty is not the essence of our relationship—our friendship is. We are not only best friends, but we are also physically attracted to each other.

People who are friends (truly good friends), tend to stay friends over long periods of time. Case in point: Who are your best friends? How long have you been friends? Have you always agreed on everything? Were you able to get beyond the things you disagreed about? The answer is "yes" and that is why you're still friends to this day. This is because you could get beyond the things you disagreed about. The same can be true for your marriage.

Some relationships start as friends and grow into love. These relationships are often among the most enduring. We have two friends, Jeffrey and Denise Hart, who were best friends in high school and continued to stay in touch during college, even though they weren't dating. They dated other people during their college years, but none of those people connected with them on a basic level of friendship like they connected with each other. Their jobs moved them to the same city, and they rekindled their friendship. Eventually, they fell in love and got married. They have had a successful marriage for over thirty years, and they still act like newlyweds.

BEFRIENDING

Successful marriages are made of friendships, plus physical attraction. But great marriages are more than good looks and good sex. If you are not married to someone who is a good friend (hopefully, your best friend), then you need to start working on improving your friendship, right now. You do that by "befriending" your spouse!

We believe to befriend someone is to intentionally reach out and to work on becoming closer to that person with a goal of becoming good or better friends. Believe it or not, you CAN become friends. This means you can develop a friendship with your spouse, even if you have had arguments and have lost some of your initial interest and loving feelings. Despite all of that, you can still create a lasting friendship that will help improve your marriage.

I believe we have all learned to like things we initially didn't care for. We see it every day. Many of us have learned to like songs we didn't like the first time we heard them. Over time, we may even come to love those songs and claim them as our own: "That's my song!" In the same way that you can learn to like a song you initially did not enjoy, you can learn to like your spouse as well. And if you learn to like them, you can go on to learn to love them.

To start this process, we recommend you study your spouse. Do you know what your spouse likes? Favorite color? Favorite food? Favorite treats? For example, I like electronic toys, so Dee gives me electronic gifts. Dee likes time and attention, and I make time for her, and give her lots of attention. I know her favorite treat is a veggie smoothie, so I will often bring her a smoothie for lunch. In terms of gifts, I know Dee does not like surprises. She would rather tell me exactly what she wants me to get her, so I ask, listen, and follow through on what she says she likes.

When we got our new bedroom furniture, I was expecting the bed linens to be white, because that's Dee's favorite color. But I was pleasantly surprised to see that she had decorated the bed with my favorite color, which is blue! If you observe and study your spouse, you can learn more about what he or she likes. It just takes time and attention! We recognize that marriage is like grass. When you see a beautiful lawn, you must understand that it didn't happen by chance. Instead, it happened through patience, care, and steady maintenance. It took time and attention.

Dee started gardening after seeing our neighbor's beautiful yard and wanted our yard to look like theirs. So, she asked our neighbor how he did it. The neighbor told Dee secrets he used, and she followed the instructions, and eventually she cultivated a beautiful garden as well. Maybe your neighbor's garden looks better than yours because it is watered and fertilized and cared for better than yours. And maybe their marriage is better than yours for similar reasons. The good news is you can learn how people who are happily married got there, and then you can do the same!

Our pastor, John K. Jenkins, Sr. and his wife of over 35 years, Trina Jenkins, share that one of their recommendations is to enter into your spouse's world. Do things your spouse likes to do. Talk about what they want to talk about. Go where they want to go. Try new experiences. He shares how he learned to like HGTV because his wife likes HGTV. And she learned to enjoy flying because he became a pilot and loves to fly. He entered into her world and she entered into his world and they learned to enjoy the new experiences. And as result, they continue to grow as friends and marriage partners!

Here are the steps to befriending your spouse:

1. **Decide. Make the decision to work on your friendship.** The first step to any achievement is to make up your mind. Decide that you are going to become great friends to each other. That might sound simplistic, but it's critical to building your relationship. Until you make that decision, nothing great is going to happen.
2. **Find something in common.** Find a similar interest or a common ground and build from there. Is it watching sports, gardening, exercising, traveling? Whatever you come up with, commit to participate together and learn more about each other as you learn more about the activity.
3. **Make a list of best friend qualities.** Each of you should make a list of what you would want to have in a best friend. Then share it with each other. Everything doesn't have to fit, but now you each know what the other is

thinking and looking for. People often marry for surface reasons, and never have had in-depth conversations. As a result, they don't know their mate's wants or desires.

4. **Study your spouse** and learn what they value, and preferences, in terms of foods, colors, hobbies, etc.

5. **Read the book** *How to Win Friends and Influence People* by Dale Carnegie. While this is a classic business book, the principles stand the test of time for building friendships. Here are ten points from the book that can help solidify your marriage friendship:

1. Listen openly (without judgment) to each other.
2. Give honest and sincere appreciation.
3. Make the other person feel important.
4. Show respect for the other person's opinion.
5. If you are wrong, admit it quickly.
6. Work at seeing things from the other person's point of view.
7. Talk about your own mistakes before criticizing the other person.
8. Let the other person save face.
9. Praise the slightest improvement and praise every improvement.
10. Use kind words, even when giving a critique.

WESTERN MARRIAGES VERSUS EASTERN MARRIAGES

We are friends with an East Indian couple, Dayal and Varkha Alwani of St. Maarten, who have been married for over forty years, and they have shared with us their observations about Western versus Eastern marriages. They believe the reason for the high divorce rate in our Western culture is because we "start off hot for each other, but cool off over time." While, in Eastern cultures, they start off cold, and get hot over time! People from their Eastern culture have arranged marriages. They must learn to like the spouses their parents chose for them to marry!

The divorce rate in Western cultures, like America and England (where we choose who we will marry), is around 50 percent. The divorce rate in Eastern cultures, like East India and Malaysia (where they have arranged marriages,) is about 5 percent. I cannot confirm scientifically that this is the reason people in Eastern cultures have such low divorce rates, but I can say that people in Western cultures often divorce because they didn't seek their parents' counsel or wise counsel in general on who they should marry. Sometimes parents can be wrong about your intended spouse, but it is good to at least seek their counsel so you can have the input of those who should know you best.

There was a TV show when I was growing up called Father Knows Best. As a father, I realize I don't always know everything, but I do share the wisdom I have gained throughout my life with my children because I hope it will help them make wiser decisions. Father and mother might not always know best, but they usually know something—and it is usually worth the time to get their opinions, so you can make a qualified decision. Listen and then decide, because ultimately it is your decision, and you must live with it. My friend Naomi Rhode shared that her father said this when she was about to get married: "Think and make good choices ... then once you make the choice, work to make your choices good." Naomi and her husband Jim, have been married for over sixty years and are not only best friends but very successful business partners. Plus, they are two of the most loving people we have ever met.

Next, I highly recommend you develop a sense of humor and be willing to laugh to diffuse conflict. Two of our closest friends are Bradley and Terry Thomas. Bradley is an attorney and also one of the funniest men I know. Terry is a nationally award-winning art school teacher. We have vacationed with them for over 30 years and have never seen them argue or have any cross words. Terry says the reason is that Bradley doesn't allow her to get angry because she's too busy laughing! We recommend you take this tip from Bradley and Terry and learn to laugh a lot!

DEE'S PERSPECTIVE

"Happy is the man who finds a true friend,
and far happier is he who finds that true friend in his wife."
~ Franz Schubert

Your best friend is the person you call first with the best or worst news. Just being around your best friend makes you feel better, safer, and more confident. You know it's all going to be alright. They celebrate with you because they understand the struggles and hurdles you've overcome. They keep your secrets. They support you. They pray for you so that you won't buckle under pressure. They even help you appear to have it all under control, like the day I lost my corporate training director's job. It was terrible, but it was a major day in the life of my relationship with Willie.

It was a cold and dreary winter day, with heavy wet snow falling so fast you could barely see the streets from my office window on the fifteenth floor. Around 1:30pm in the afternoon, my boss called me into his office. I thought we were being dismissed early due to the horrible weather conditions. Instead, I found out I was being fired.

The corporation was downsizing and the insurance division that housed my training department was being eliminated. I learned that day that training and development departments were not revenue generating, meaning they were the first to be eliminated in the face of economic challenges.

To make matters worse, my boss, the company's vice president, said, "I never really liked you anyway. You remind me of my ex-wife. (How horrible was that!!!???) Clean out your desk. Human Resources will contact you in the next few days to discuss your severance package." I was dazed. I stumbled back to my office and tried to collect my thoughts. I thought to myself, "I am a single woman in D.C. I drive a Datsun 280Z sports car that belongs to the bank, I rent an expensive condo on the swanky upper Northwest side, and losing this job means I am a few months from financial ruin." Ouch.

Calling my parents was out of the question. I could not have them worry. I was a big girl now and my pride said l should not call them for help. They had paid for my undergraduate education, and I had gone on to get an advanced degree. I had all the trappings of the high life, but on an overextended budget. Under the circumstances, I decided to call my best friend. "Willie, please meet me at my apartment. I've been fired."

The snow was almost blinding. As I inched my way up Connecticut Avenue, I heard a special news announcement on the radio: "Air Florida Boeing 727 Flight 90 just crashed. It hit the 14th Street Bridge and then went into the icy Potomac River!" It was 4:01p.m. on January 13, 1982. Seventy-eight people, including four who were in their vehicles on the 14th

Street Bridge, died that day.

Somehow, I made it home and Willie was waiting in the lobby. We said nothing to each other at that moment. His presence was all that was necessary. We decided to walk to the Giant Food store to get supplies for the storm. Holding hands, we trudged up the Connecticut Avenue hill as we spoke softly of the horrors of the plane crash and took in the sights of sliding cars.

Willie had become my best friend, and I was so happy he was there. We had been dating regularly since the fall of 1981. We shared the same views on life. He got me to laugh; I had previously had no sense of humor. He lifted my spirits and made me feel the world would right itself again. In short, he gave me hope.

I believe that is what great friends do. From that great friendship we established the foundation for a great marriage. Over thirty years later, we are still great friends, as well as great marriage partners. Friends first! Please make a point to marry someone who is your great friend.

Go Beyond Your Personal Comfort Zone

I had to be willing to go beyond my comfort zone, to learn more about Willie and his world. I was from Hampton Virginia, a seafood town, yet I had never eaten hard shell crabs. I didn't even know how to open them. Willie loved crabs and would open them for me. He also loved sushi, and I had only eaten fish that was cooked. Yet, I learned to love sushi as well. Plus, I was not a jazz music lover, I only listened to gospel music and talk radio. I had never purchased a record in my life, yet I was falling in love with a person who loved jazz and many different types of music. He listened to music all the time and sang in jazz clubs. As a preacher's kid, I had never set foot in a night club and now I was going into these loud, dark, smoke filled places where people were playing music that I didn't even understand. But, Willie was my best friend. I wanted to know more about his world. As a result, he gave me a gift of real-life classes in music appreciation. I have come to appreciate different styles of music and have learned to open a crab on my own!

Be open to sharing new experiences as you build your friendship. Explore and stretch beyond your comfort zone. Create new memories together as you learn to appreciate their thinking and what they value.

♥ JOLLEY ADVICE

1. **Learn to like your spouse—over, over and over again.** Think about what attracted you in the first place and remind yourself and each other of those qualities—all the time.

2. **Focus on what you have in common—not the differences.** Every person comes with ideas, thoughts, and positions that are imprinted from their parents and the environment they grew up in. Many of these are hard wired. Change may not happen quickly, and sometimes it won't happen at all. Focus on what you have in common more than what you don't have in common.

3. **Talk about what you value. Practice articulating what is important to each of you. Listen more than you talk.**

4. **Laugh together. Friends share humor and laughter.** The Bible says in Proverbs that "laughter is good medicine."

5. **Hold hands.** It might sound corny, but it works! Holding hands keeps the friendship and the affection going.

6. **Tell everyone that you're married to your best friend.**
Say it often, because as you speak, so shall it become.

7. **Be Friends!!!!**

> *For those not yet married, make sure to see
> the resource section at the end of the book for
> tips on choosing the right person to marry!*

♥

CHAPTER TWO

Make God an Equal Part in Your Marriage

"Marriage takes three to be complete.
If you involve the Creator, it can be oh so sweet!"
~ Anonymous

WILLIE'S PERSPECTIVE

I love the quote that reads, *"If success is truly meant to be, it takes a combination of three—husband, wife & Thee (God)."* The author is anonymous, but whoever wrote this, is right on target. Dee and I believe that God needs to be an equal part of your union. This is a step we have found essential to a successful marriage. After being best friends, make sure you are friends with God and that He is in the mix of your marriage and your decisions. You will need His insights and wisdom along the way. In fact, we believe that God actually is the majority owner of the marriage!

We believe that marriage is a triangle with God at the top angle and the couple at the bottom corner angles. If you look at the total area of the triangle as covering 100%, and there are three angles, then it is divided into 33%, 33% and 34%. We see the husband at the left corner of the triangle, with 33%. The wife would be the right corner of the triangle with 33%.

That would leave the top angle which would be 34%, and that is God's portion. Meaning, God has the majority percentage of the marriage. The husband and the wife are equal, neither having a bigger percentage than the other. Therefore, we believe every major decision needs to be run by the majority partner—God!

When you involve the majority owner in decisions, your life will be much easier. God created principles for marriage that are located in His book, the Bible. Whether you are a believer or not, the principles work. My friend, Pastor Dante King, shared this quote with me that sums it up: "If you walk by God's principles, you will have less need for miracles!" We have found this to be absolutely true.

THE IMPORTANCE OF WISDOM IN MARRIAGE

Marriage success takes wisdom. In Webster's Dictionary, wisdom is defined as "the ability to understand and do what is proper and reasonable, to have good sense, to discern inner qualities and relationships." I like to say that wisdom is to get clarity on what to do, when you don't know what to do. It is to have good judgment in difficult moments. Difficult moments in marriage are situations and circumstances that pop up where you genuinely do not know what to do. Great wisdom for these moments is best found in the principles and precepts of God, especially the principles found in the book of Proverbs. With that wisdom you will avoid foolish decisions that could negatively impact your future. That is why we say you need to have God as a major partner in your marriage.

When Dee and I were dating, I was co-parenting my ten-year-old daughter. She would spend summers and holidays with me and school time with her mom. When my daughter met Dee, they immediately became great friends. They did everything together—that is, until the day that Dee and I got married! Once we got married, my daughter became a terror. She became difficult and divisive. I learned that while my daughter was comfortable with Dee when we were dating, she had been told, and had accepted, the old wives' tale that step-moms are mean and nasty.

Once Dee and I were married, my daughter felt that I would forget about her, and she reacted negatively. When my daughter changed, it was very difficult for Dee, because it seemed to come out of the blue. It was certainly one of the worst times in my life, when it should have been one of the happiest times in my life. I had a daughter I loved, and a wife I loved, so it should have been wonderful. Instead, I had something that felt like I was going through hell—two people who each wanted me to take their side. I was in the middle, literally stuck between a rock and a hard place. I didn't know what to do. I needed help! I needed wisdom!

The book of Proverbs tells us repeatedly that there is safety in a multitude of counselors, and that we should seek wisdom from the wise. I decided to go to the wisest person I knew, who also happened to be the person who had always been there for me, my mother, Catherine Jolley. She had never personally experienced anything like this, because when she married my dad neither of them had children from a previous relationship. She told me she wouldn't give me a theoretical solution to my problem. Rather, she told me to do what she did when she didn't know what to do, which was to pray for wisdom. Mom told me that she and my dad would pray for wisdom in their marriage and in raising me and my brother.

I followed her advice and prayed, asking God to give me wisdom and direction. God answered my prayer by teaching me insights to help my daughter feel secure while also making

Dee comfortable and confident in this new arrangement as a mom to a teenage daughter. With time, things started to change, and our situation got better.

With that, I realized scripture is true—wisdom is the primary thing. Before you seek anything else, get wisdom! It is necessary in every facet of life. I prayed for wisdom and I got wise answers. It was a gift from God, and it's not just for me. This gift is available to everyone, and the secret is that you must be willing to ask for it. You must be willing to pray, and then take positive action. But the key action is to read and learn the principles and precepts that God has offered to us in His word.

Dee and I decided to seek wisdom in every part of our lives, which certainly included our marriage. There have been many times over the years when we didn't know what to do, but we sought God's wisdom and were given the answers. We now know that one of the keys to our marriage success is to consult God, our majority partner. As a result, our marriage has gotten better and better, sweeter and sweeter, each and every year.

The great theologian Reinhold Niebuhr wrote a poem that talks about the importance of Godly wisdom in our lives. He wrote:

O God, grant me the serenity to accept the things I cannot change,
Courage to change the things I can,
And wisdom to know the difference.

We recommend you make God an equal part of your marriage; and that you pray for wisdom and involve God in your decisions. Do that and you will see that it will help to strengthen your marriage.

To involve God in your decisions, pray for wisdom, and then make it a habit to pray without ceasing. That may sound like a tall order when you're so busy, but you don't have to be physically on your knees every moment of the day to pray without ceasing. You do it by having an ongoing 24/7 heart that is open to God. It is a position of gratitude and thankfulness. It is being in a spirit where we are communicating with God at all times.

It is like the old story of two monks in the early 1900s who were talking about smoking while praying. One said to the other, "I went to the Holy Father and asked if I could smoke while I was praying, and he said "Absolutely not!" The other said he too went to the Holy Father and asked if he could pray while he was smoking, and the answer he got was, "Absolutely yes!" The same can be said of how we communicate with God in the midst of our busy lives. Do we need to stop and fall on our knees every moment when we are dealing with our spouses? No! But we should develop a relationship with God in which we are constantly and consistently communicating, being grateful and open to His insights and direction. Even though I am not with you as you read this book, I am grateful that you picked it up and started reading it, because I know that it will save some marriages and strengthen others. If I were with you right now, I would proclaim again that you should seek wisdom and make God an equal partner in your marriage. You will be glad you did!

DEE'S PERSPECTIVE

Willie and I share the same Christian beliefs, based on our faith in Jesus Christ. Because we share that faith, when we got married, we agreed to be governed by God's principles as instructed in the Bible.

According to the Word, the man is the head of the household. I gave a lot of thought to this before we married. Was I supposed to follow Willie, as the head of our household, as he follows Christ? What?! Could I allow myself to be submitted to his authority? I'd been living on my own for more than ten years! What might submitting to his authority look like? What level of influence would or could I exert in this kind of relationship?

Willie and I talked it through and discussed different scenarios. What if I disagreed with his decisions? How would we resolve matters? The Bible would be the governing tool, and Willie gently reminded me that I just needed to make him feel he that he was in charge! "You run everything anyway, I'm comfortable with that," he said. "But, you must at least let me think I am in charge!" Since we study under the same ministry, and share the same values, I thought being on the same page with our thinking would be easy. It turned out that wasn't the case, specifically, when it came to raising children, and especially as it related to our blended family.

I married a man with a daughter, and I thought my relationship with Sherry was great. She traveled with me and visited with my mom and dad often. Portions of her summer vacations were spent with me. We got along well—that is, until Willie and I said I do. That's when I learned the power of the veto. I had agreed that if Willie and I had a stalemate, we would pray and Willie would make the final call.

The test came on a Wednesday afternoon. Sherry had set up a rendezvous with her mom to help rescue her from us. She wanted to be free from our "prison"—free from wearing a school uniform, free from having a curfew, free from doing her homework on time, and free from not being allowed to date without a chaperone.

Frankly, I thought Sherry's departure was wonderful. Peace and harmony were now restored in our household. But it lasted only a few months. An evening call from Sherry's mom shattered all of that. She said Sherry was skipping school, involved with the wrong crowd, smoking, and wouldn't do anything she told her to do. Therefore, she needed Willie to come get her ASAP!

I was not in support of that and told Willie in no uncertain terms. There was no agreement on my part about him going to rescue her. Her mother had made the bed, so I felt we should let her lie in it.

Willie felt we needed to go get her. He said it was the right thing to do, but I objected. So, I sought wise counsel. Well, in reality, I complained to my mom as the situation unfolded. I wanted her sympathy, but her simple question brought me back to my proper position in my marriage. My mom asked, "Would you want to be married to a man who wouldn't do everything possible to save his child from self-destruction?" Of course, the answer was no. "Well, you put yourself in that car with him and go get that child! You work with him and support him as he builds his parenting relationship with his daughter. It's hard work to go from being a fun-loving buddy to being the authority figure in the household. Your role is to support and provide wise counsel – ever so gently! And, remember, choose your words with care." All I could say was, "Yes, ma'am." I did not want to hear those words of wisdom, but I knew she was right. I also knew my home environment was going to get very uncomfortable.

The next day we got in the car to take that five-hour drive to pick up Sherry. Willie and I spoke very little. Frankly, I was sad. How was I going to be the thoughtful, kind, loving spouse who worked nine to five, drove children to school, chaperoned school events, cooked evening meals, helped with the homework, supervised the house chores, prepared for couples' date night all while feeling trapped with a person who did not like me? We were bringing this unpleasant person back into my sanctuary.

The Bible says that the prayers of the righteous avail much. I knew my mom and dad were praying for me and Willie. Willie was praying for wisdom and I was praying for strength. Plus, the Sunday sermons as well as the Bible studies we attended had provided me with the knowledge of how to think and what to do. Now was the hard work of implementing it, and I just didn't feel like doing it. It was too hard. I recalled sermons that said, "Love them even when they don't love you! In fact, love them first!" But my stepdaughter called me "she." How was I supposed to love such a person first? "Does your stepmother have a name?" the counselor asked her. Apparently not to Sherry!

I felt like I had gone the extra mile, even as far as adding her to my health insurance plan. I drove her to school and helped her with her hobbies and activities. I bought her school clothes that her mother said she didn't have to wear. All of this and I was supposed to love her first?!

As I sat in that passenger seat on the ride to retrieve Sherry, I was not happy. But I knew my mom was right. The only thing that could change was me. It was the wisdom of God that my mom extended to me, and I decided to act like what God had called us to do—love first! But how was I going to manage that love and compassion for her that I did not feel?

To act with the love and compassion for her that I didn't feel, I created this scenario that I played over and over and over again in my head: If I had passed away and Willie remarried, my young son would be raised by Willie's next wife—his stepmother. How would I want that stepmother to treat my baby boy? And what would happen if William had a bad attitude and the same behavior that Sherry was exhibiting now? Wouldn't I want the stepmom to be patient and kind to William? I would want her to be loving like Jesus, forgiving like Job, encouraging like Paul, and always teaching and going the extra mile for my baby boy. That's when I realized I had to be that too!

We arrived, and the conversations were forced pleasantries. We took Sherry home, and it was tough. She was angry, rebellious, and rude, yet Willie maintained his calm and never responded in kind. He was consistent in shaping her thinking and shaping the culture we were going to have as a family. In time, she came around and things did change, and she and I developed a good relationship.

Today, we are very close and every time we talk, she again thanks us for loving her when she was unlovable. If Willie had not exercised his veto when I wanted to leave her and forget about her, there would not have been a happy ending to this story.

I recommend wives mediate on Proverbs 31, about the virtuous woman, to help activate your faith, which I know helps the wife do her part to build a strong loving marriage. It reads:

A good woman is hard to find, and worth far more than diamonds.

Her husband trusts her without reserve, and never has reason to regret it.

Never spiteful, she treats him generously all her life long.

She shops around for the best yarns and cottons, and enjoys knitting and sewing.

She's like a trading ship that sails to faraway places and brings back exotic surprises.

She's up before dawn, preparing breakfast for her family and organizing her day.

She looks over a field and buys it, then, with money she's put aside, plants a garden.

First thing in the morning, she dresses for work, rolls up her sleeves, eager to get started.

She senses the worth of her work, is in no hurry to call it quits for the day.

She's skilled in the crafts of home and hearth, diligent in homemaking.

She's quick to assist anyone in need, reaches out to help the poor.

She doesn't worry about her family when it snows; their winter clothes are all mended and ready to wear.

She makes her own clothing, and dresses in colorful linens and silks.

Her husband is greatly respected when he deliberates with the city fathers.

She designs gowns and sells them, brings the sweaters she knits to the dress shops.

Her clothes are well-made and elegant, and she always faces tomorrow with a smile.

When she speaks she has something worthwhile to say, and she always says it kindly.

She keeps an eye on everyone in her household, and keeps them all busy and productive.

Her children respect and bless her; her husband joins in with words of praise:

'Many women have done wonderful things, but you've outclassed them all!'

Charm can mislead and beauty soon fades.

The woman to be admired and praised is the woman who lives in the Fear-of-GOD.

Give her everything she deserves! Festoon her life with praises!

Proverbs 31:10–31 (MSG)

Be the kind of woman that walks by faith, so when your feet hit the floor every morning, the devil says, "Oh No! She's

Up! There she goes, fighting for her family!"

Willie recommends husbands meditate on this scripture:

> *Husbands, go all out in your love for your wives, exactly as Christ did for the church—a love marked by giving, not getting. Christ's love makes the church whole. His words evoke her beauty. Everything he does and says is designed to bring the best out of her, dressing her in dazzling white silk, radiant with holiness." And that is how husbands ought to love their wives. They're really doing themselves a favor—since they're already "one" in marriage.*
> *Ephesians 5:25–28 (MSG)*

♥ JOLLEY ADVICE

1. **Memorize the phrase WWJD (What Would Jesus Do?).** We recommend you adopt that phrase in your marriage and ask, "What Would Jesus Do?" Think about what He would do, especially when you are having issues. Then do it.

2. **Talk about your faith and pray together.** People say that the family who prays together, stays together. It might sound corny, but let us tell you, it works.

3. **Pray for each other. Pray for your spouse daily.** When you have challenges, pray for wisdom.

4. **Love each other as God loves us!** God has it figured out—just do it His way. Husbands, love your wives and treat them like Christ treated the church. He was willing to die for the church, and there is no greater love than that. And wives, love your husbands by encouraging them and supporting them.

5. **Share uplifting materials with each other.** Input determines output. After you read a good book, share it with your spouse. That way you will grow together, and neither will become stagnant in the relationship. Set your sights on learning and growing together, both mentally and spiritually.

6. **Trust God!** Life—and marriage—require trust and confidence in God. Keep talking to Him, listening, and sharing His word and principles with each other as well as others in your network.

7. **We recommend you read one Proverb per day.** There are 31—one for each day of the month.

♥

CHAPTER THREE

Decide to Make it Last

"Getting married is easy. Staying married is more difficult. Staying happily married for a lifetime should rank among the fine arts."
~ Roberta Flack

LOVE IS AN EMOTION, BUT MARRIAGE IS A DECISION!

Most people think that long-term happy marriages happen only because you fall in love. That is not true, because it takes much more than just falling in love. Our friend, Dr. George Fraser, CEO of the Power Networking Conference, has been married for over 40 years and says, "You meet and fall in love by chance, but you stay in love by choice!"

WILLIE'S PERSPECTIVE

We have found that, unfortunately, most people get married because they fall "in-like" and think it is love, and over time that emotion changes. We believe that falling in love is just the first step to a long and happy marriage. Two people must make a conscious decision (which is the process of making up your minds), and actually commit to staying together. You must decide to stay married and then work to make that decision a reality.

Falling in love is easy. Some people love to fall in love, so they fall in love repeatedly to experience the wonderful feeling. I have a friend who enjoys falling in love and does so every couple of months! He's constantly in new relationships. He is addicted to the thrill of falling in love. But after that thrill fades, he falls out of love just as quickly as he fell in love. As easy and fun as falling in love can be, the other extreme, falling out of love or being in love with someone who has fallen out of love with you, can be very painful. The Righteous Brothers sang of the pain of being in a relationship where their mate fell out of love. They sang, "You've lost that loving feeling…it's gone, gone, gone!" And popular R & B singer, Raphael Saadiq sang, "Falling in love is so easy! Staying in love is too tricky!"

We've discovered that when you have a great marriage, you are constantly falling in love; and rather than falling out of love, you are always in an evolving, growing, and flowing love experience. In other words, you are always falling in love, but it's with the same person! Dee and I are continually adding new layers to our current loving relationship. We were more deeply in love at the thirty-year mark than we were at the one-year mark. Why? We've been through many trials and challenges together, and we know we can trust each other with our inner most thoughts and fears. We look to each other for wise counsel during the darkest hours, knowing if no one else comes to save us, we've got each other's backs—along with God. I tell her often, "You know what…you turn me on!" And the interesting thing is that I am not lying! It's like fine wine, it just gets better with time.

DECIDE

Marriage, and staying married, is a decision. The word

decision is taken from the root word "cision," which means "to cut." If you make an "in-cision," you cut in, and if you make a "de-cision," you cut off. Therefore, when you make a decision, you are cutting off the options that would allow you to go in a different direction. You decide to stay the course and do whatever is necessary to succeed with that chosen avenue. Therefore, getting married should not be a flippant decision. I would not recommend that it be a spur of the moment choice, made after a night of drinking and other revelries. Nor should it be a decision made just because you had a few good times. This is serious and should be considered and thought about in great detail.

When we were newly married, I visited a neighboring couple who had been married for over fifty years. They were two of the nicest people I had ever met. Mr. Benson helped everyone in the neighborhood and his wife made the best cookies you have ever tasted. They were a wonderful couple and were often seen in the evening going for a walk and holding hands. I sat with Mr. Benson on his front porch and asked what I needed to do to be able to be happily married like he was. He pondered for a second and said, "It's a decision. Most people are simply not willing to make the decision. You stood before the preacher or the justice of the peace and you were asked if you would take her as your wife. You said that you do. Now, you simply need to DO!" This was a great lesson. It has been one of the bedrock lessons of my life, and one I often share in my programs when I talk about "Mentors versus Mistakes." I explain that there are two ways to learn anything: mentors and mistakes. Both will get you to the goal, but one gets you there with fewer headaches and heartaches. I recommend you get mentors who have successfully done what you want to do, and learn from them.

I was listening to a radio program and heard the host give advice to a listener who was having marital problems. The radio host had been married a few times, and he gave the advice he had followed in his prior marriages: "When things get tough, you should just leave!" I was astonished. Let me say unequivocally: No! I don't agree! If you leave every time you have a problem in a relationship, you will never develop the skills to work through difficult situations. Marriage success is skilled based. Sooner or later things, get tough in every marriage. To achieve success, you will need to develop the skills to stay married early on, and keep refining them over time.

One key to our success is that Dee and I decided that divorce was not an option, not even on the table for consideration. When we married, I told Dee this was it, and the only way we could get out of it was to die.

Since divorce could not even be considered, we had no choice but to work it out. Early on in our marriage, when we had rough moments, this commitment was particularly relevant. We kept working, and working through every challenging situation that came up. If you are committed, you will keep working on problems until you fix them. It's a process, and you should never short circuit the process by running to a divorce lawyer. Just like the couple who had been married for over fifty years told us: "You made a promise and said I do. Now do!" We pass that same advice on to you. You said "I do!" Now do!

COMMITMENT

Once you make the decision to stay married, you must make a commitment to that decision. The commitment is necessary because feelings change. Our love for each other has changed over the years. It is not static, nor is it stagnant. It moves, flows, and changes. In fact, our marriage has continued to change for the better.

While giving a television interview, I commented that I actually love Dee more now than I did when we got married! I loved her a lot when we got married, partly because it was new and exciting. But now I know her better. I've experienced her standing with me through the toughest moments of my life. She was by my side with each and every business venture I tried. Some succeeded, some failed. But through them all, she stood by me. She stood by me when my mother, my brother, and her father died within thirty days of each other. She could have said, "I can't deal with your issues because I have my own issues to deal with." But she did not say that. She said, "We are in this together and we will work through it." We held on to each other through the three funerals where I eulogized my mom, my brother, and her father. These times were tough, but together we got through it. These experiences have helped to make our love stronger now than it was when we first married.

As Dee and I did, you must make a commitment to that commitment. The promise plus the commitment are a critical part of the marriage success formula. If you make the commitment to not just "go" through the challenges of life and marriage, but to "grow" through the challenges, you will be amazed at what you can accomplish as a couple. The dividends will be well worth the investments you make, allowing you to enjoy the future fruits of a great marriage.

COMMITMENTS VERSUS GOALS

In seminars, I teach about the power of goals. A goal is an aim, a target that you set to help you accomplish a specific task. And one of the key points about effectively setting goals is to accomplish the task in a specific time frame. In fact, goals should be S.M.A.R.T.: Specific, Measurable, Achievable,

Relevant, and Time Bound.

Goals are tools I use to help me hit my targets. But sometimes I don't hit the goal in the time I had hoped. Let's say, for example, I set a goal to generate a certain amount of money, and I don't achieve it this year, or next year, or the next. Nevertheless, I keep working at it. Goals are meant to help achieve a certain task. If you miss the goal, you try again. When you miss your goal, it is not the end of the world… no big deal; but if you break a promise, it's a huge deal.

Here is an example of the difference. Every year, thirty-two professional football teams set a goal to win the NFL's annual Super Bowl. Only one team can achieve that goal. The rest missed the mark for that year, but they all set the same goal the next year. They do not promise that they will win the Super Bowl; they set a goal and their fans join in to support them in their efforts to achieve that goal. Even when the team misses the goal of winning the Super Bowl, the fans continue to buy tickets.

But what if a team promised to win the Super Bowl and then didn't do it? Do you think their fans would continue to support them year after year with them breaking their promise? The obvious answer is no, certainly not. The team would lose support if they kept breaking their promise. That is why a promise is more powerful than a goal. When you don't hit a goal, you reset it. But when you break a promise, you break a heart. When you get married, you are not setting a goal but making a promise. That is what vows are about—they are promises meant to be kept.

Have you ever really listened to the traditional marriage vows? They read, "I, _____, take you, _____, to be my lawfully wedded (husband/wife), to have and to hold from this day forward, for better, for worse, for richer, for poorer, in sickness and in health, to love and to cherish, till death us do part, according to God's holy law, and this is my solemn vow." That is not a hope statement., as in, "I hope to stay married." Rather it is a promise: "I promise to stay married."

In the wedding vows the line "for better or worse" is more than just words, it is also a decision on commitment. We ask couples a question about this line when they are considering getting married: "The wedding vows say you take each other for richer or poorer, for better or for worse, until death do us part, so what would you consider to be worse?" Most people say unfaithfulness would be worse. I always ask them if they are really willing to do what they vow, stay for better or for worse, and then I share a story about my former neighbors.

This family lived a few doors up from my family when I was growing up. They had four children who were my playmates. Years later, I would occasionally ride through the neighborhood and see the husband and wife sitting on the porch holding hands. I would stop and greet them and they would share that they were doing fine and dandy.

When the husband died, I was asked to speak at his funeral, and that's when I learned that the husband had been unfaithful. He had two additional children from women who lived in the neighborhood, yet his wife had stayed with him. She said she made a vow to take him for better for worse and she stayed with him, through the worse, until his death thirty-five years later.

They worked through the pain of "worse" and were able to stay together through it. And as a result, they were able to enjoy their autumn years and sit on a porch and hold hands together. For better, for worse: Better is easy. Worse can be very, very difficult. Are you truly ready and willing to work through the worse?

Occasionally, we see couples who marry and say they will TRY to make it work. My response to them is always the same. I pull a pen out of my pocket and put it on a table. Then I ask them to pick it up. Then I say, "put it down." Then I ask them to NOT pick it up. Therefore they don't pick it up and so they cannot put it down. Finally, I ask them to TRY and pick it up, and once they do, I have them. The point is that you either do or don't—you don't merely try. Marriage is similar. You don't try, you do! And that takes a commitment to keep working through your challenges. It is not a hope or a wish or a try—it is a do! And that takes commitment.

A friend of our son contacted him and asked if she could talk to us for advice on a situation she was having. She shared that she'd gotten married right out of college. She was soon pregnant and had a baby. Her husband took a new position with a significant pay raise. Therefore, he suggested she could stay at home, if she liked, so she could enjoy more time with the baby. But she was not happy. She felt she was missing all the fun her friends were talking about. Many of her friends were still enjoying the single life. She missed partying and being free and single. Her friends made their dating adventures seem so exciting, while she felt she was living a boring life. She complained about it and told us she wanted to leave him because it looked fun to be single and active.

I shared that the single life she saw from the viewpoint of her friends was a myth. It goes along with the myth that the grass is greener on the other side. The truth is that when you get to the other side, you find the green grass is artificial turf. It looks good from afar, but when you scrape up against it, you realize it hurts.

The grass is not greener on the other side. It is a mistake to look at someone else's life and make a judgment about your own. A distant view of a friend's life is not the measure used to throw away a husband, a baby, and a marriage. Many have fallen for that myth and lived the rest of their lives in misery.

COMPROMISE

We live in Washington, D.C., where politicians often act like compromise is a bad word. But in terms of marriage, I assure you that compromise is a great word. Smart business people understand the power of compromise, and smart people in marriages understand it too. Compromise, by its definition, is "a settlement agreement which is reached by mutual concessions of both parties." We've seen that the marriages that succeed are the marriages where there is the ability to compromise. Sometimes the wife gets her way, sometimes the husband gets his way, and sometimes they meet in the middle, and keep it moving. I had the honor of doing some events with Dr. Stephen Covey, the author of The 7 Habits of Highly Effective People. He wrote that one of the most important habits was "win/win." Not only it is important in business, but also in marriage. I heard NBC Weatherman Al Roker say on TV one morning that one of the keys to his long marriage was to understand that neither person has to be right all the time. It is win/win!

Our friends, the Bermans, call it "sharing the power." We had dinner with Sanford and Linda Berman, who have been married for almost 50 years. What is interesting is that Sanford is one of the top divorce lawyers in America. He said many of the people who come to him to get a divorce complain about how their spouse would not compromise. Sanford said he thinks that many could have avoided a divorce if they would just share the power. He has learned over the years that marriage is about sharing: sharing the power, the money, the responsibilities, the household chores, and even sharing the good and the bad.

When we interviewed Bill and Vivian Clark, who are lifelong friends of ours, we asked what the secret was to their ability to get married while in college and then live successfully together for over forty years. They looked at each other and in unison responded: "compromise and being conciliatory." Bill said he lives by this edict: "Work it out and fix the feelings—fast!" Vivian says, "Don't let things linger and don't hold grudges."

Neither of you is going to be right all the time, so you must compromise. As my friend Zemira Jones says, "Don't stamp collect." That means don't hold on to anger, grudges, and hurt feelings, waiting for a later date to drop all those negative emotions to get back at the other person.

You can develop a mindset to compromise and succeed more by asking a simple question: Do I want to win this argument, or do I want to be happy? Which one do you want more? Those who choose being at peace and having more happiness at home are those who have figured it out and are able to spend their time living better and more fulfilling lives.

DEE'S PERSPECTIVE

My friend, Carolyn, chuckled, almost to herself, as she passed by our bedroom as we headed downstairs from seeing the renovations to our second floor. "You've fallen apart," she said. Carolyn has been my girlfriend for over forty years. She saved me from the brink of homelessness when I was fired from my training director position and could no longer afford the rent for my Connecticut Avenue condo. Carolyn invited me to move into to her spare room on Taussig Place in Northeast D.C. That's where I began to deal with the shame of losing my job, a job that defined who I was, and figure out how to go on with my life—namely, how to conduct a job search and work on developing a closer friendship with my best friend Willie.

Carolyn said, "When you were single, you were so particular about your bed linens matching, pillows positioned just so, and keeping your clothes and shoes in drawers and closets. What happened?" "I got married!" I exclaimed. I'd moved from fluffy white linens with tucked hospital corner sheets and a white satin bedspread with matching pillow covers, to a bed not made up at all, at least on Willie's side. Willie didn't grasp the concept. "Why make up the bed? You're just going to get back in it later." "Oh my" I said to myself." I was traumatized...I couldn't believe what I was hearing! Yet, we worked it out and now have a bed and linens we both enjoy.

Some might say that making up your bed is an insignificant detail in the greater sense of relationship development, but not for me. The condition of my home—the kitchen, the bedrooms, my closets—all helped define me. Organization made me feel happy and secure. I was organized to a fault. The refrigerator had only glass containers for the leftovers. I uncluttered my closets monthly to relax. I loved to fold the freshly laundered towels and stack them by color in the closets. The under-the-counter cabinets in the bathrooms were straightened weekly—paper towel to the right, toilet paper to the left, soaps in the middle. I thrived on attention to detail and minimalism. I think they call it being "anal-retentive." And I was so happy with it all!

After saying "I do" to Willie, I realized our views on housekeeping were drastically different. Coming home to an unmade bed, tripping over shoes in the middle of our bedroom floor, closet doors left wide open, and laundry on the floor was enough to push me over the edge. I felt this was not the recipe for a happy marriage. I didn't know what to do.

I mulled over my thoughts for several days, praying for wisdom. I knew I needed to select the right words to use before

I approached Willie about this situation. Eventually, I spoke of how the messy room made me feel. I didn't nag, holler, or scream, and, to his credit, he listened intently. He didn't realize that it bothered me so much. I suggested a compromise that would make us both smile when we entered our bedroom, which I considered our sanctuary, and I outlined the rewards he would receive for doing his part.

Carolyn saw the result of that compromise the evening she was visiting with us. Gone was the pressed white satin bedspread with the hospital corner sheets tucked between the mattress and box spring. A navy blue duvet cover, which Willie loved, was now in its place. Gone were the fluffy white pillows with the beaded tassels. In their place were big colorful pillows piled in the center of the bed, meant to make bed organizing easier for Willie. A long bed skirt meant tennis shoes, cycling cleats, water bottles, and other items could be pushed under the bed and out of my sight. Plus, the agreement that all Willie had to do was hide his clothes in the closet—unhung if he wanted—with shoes and other debris under the bed, so I would not trip over them, would be enough to get him a reward of his choice, whenever he wanted it! And he was always overjoyed with the same reward—which he did not have to initiate—sex! Oh, the power of positive reinforcement. So much sweeter than nagging!

The lesson here is to find out what turns each other on and supply it. That is what comes from talking to each other honestly and openly about everything. Then each person must freely decide to provide what the other wants. In exchange for providing what your spouse wants and needs to feel comfortable, you get what you want and need.

DECIDE

Decide is a powerful action word. It means to consciously and deliberately choose something. My example about our bedroom is a simple one, but it's typical of the kind of issues common in marriage. I decided I needed to change my attitude toward how I viewed our bedroom! Once I was able to make the mental adjustment, the physical redesign of the space was a breeze.

Deciding of my own free will was powerful for me. At the same time, when I decided to jump in the boat with Willie for life, I really had no clue where it would take me. My commitment to Willie has taken me all over the world, including foreign lands like Lagos, Nigeria. I still remember sitting in the tiny Lagos Airline lounge, the size of two bathroom stalls put together, waiting for a return flight to Washington, D.C. The words of Ruth, the Moabite from the Bible, came to me: "Entreat me not to leave you. For your people shall be my people and your God my God!" While Ruth originally spoke those words to her mother-in-law, Naomi, the concept was applicable to me too. I had decided to be by Willie's side, and that meant traveling. But at that moment in the airport, I'd had to have a much-needed pep talk with myself. Between the lack of air conditioning and the multiple bumpy road trips to Willie's conference site, I had to adjust my attitude. The situation was compounded by the rushing back and forth between the airport and our hotel as we tried to catch a standby flight to make it home in time for a friend's funeral in the States. I wondered to myself, how I had ended up here. But I immediately realized I had decided to—I'd made a choice! I had considered all my alternatives and made up my mind logically and emotionally that Willie would be the one for me. From that point forward, I had worked hard to make my decision the right one.

One early major test of my commitment to marry Willie was moving into his mother's attic. That was not a part of my plan. I wanted to get an apartment. Willie felt that we should save that rent money to buy a house, so he convinced me to live in his mother's attic to save money. He promised me that if we lived in the attic for a year, he'd figure out how to buy us a house. I decided to agree, but it was awfully hard for me to adjust. I'd owned a home, rented a fancy condo and now I was being asked to live in an attic with a bathroom one-flight down. When I considered my alternatives, I had to work through my emotions, many of which were selfish and self-absorbed. Then I decided to "get in the boat" with Willie and live in the attic. A year later, just as he had promised, we purchased and moved into our own home. This experience helped to build the trust in our relationship. We agreed to work together for a specific outcome and made it happen.

Today, we're still working together. We're together at least twenty hours out of each day, but we have different morning routines. I'm at the gym by 5:45 a.m. while he sleeps in and then heads for the gym around 8:00 a.m. Our offices are on opposite sides of our business's reception area. When he's on tour, I'm on tour with him. When he's writing, I edit. When he networks, I provide follow-up. There are last-minute networking affairs, often unexpected, people drop in to visit and often stay for dinner. Willie is in constant motion and always has something going on.

How do we make this chaos work for us? We decide to make it work! I'm committed to the decision I made—for better or worse, in the United States or not, through crazy times and calm times. I honor the choice I made and work on it one surprise after another. After more than thirty years of marriage, even with the messy bedroom decor, it is the best decision of my life after my commitment to Jesus Christ.

One Important Caveat – In this chapter we have stressed the importance of working through your differences and deciding to stay together through the challenges, yet we must make one exception...domestic violence! Domestic violence is never acceptable! Ever!!! If your spouse is abusive, we recommend you get help immediately. Do not delay! Call the National Domestic Violence Hotline (1-800-799-7233).

♥ JOLLEY ADVICE

1. Make a verbal commitment to each other that you will stay married.
2. Declare to each other and to the world that divorce is not an option.
3. Find a happily married couple to be your mentors.
4. Do not ask people who are not happily married for marital advice.
5. Be willing to compromise...often!
6. Discuss "For Better & For Worse" and what it means to each of you and how you would handle "worse!"
7. If you ever experience domestic violence...get help immediately!

♥

CHAPTER FOUR

Communicate! Talk to Each Other

"Communication in marriage is like oil in your automobile engine, it can be messy to handle, but without it your engine will run poorly and eventually lock up and bust! So keep talking!"
~ Dr. Willie Jolley

Communication, or the lack thereof, can make or break a marriage. Studies repeatedly reveal that communication is one of the top issues that break up marriages. A happy marriage requires open, honest, and loving communication.

WILLIE'S PERSPECTIVE

When Dee and I were first married, an older couple told us this about communication: "You must talk to each other and must talk about everything—the good, the bad, the ugly, and the uncomfortable. Don't assume anything. You did not marry a mind reader!" This advice not only helped us, but it has also helped the many couples we have shared it with. The reason for that is simple: Communication is one of the most critical areas of marriage, and when it's done well, it can enhance and grow a marriage and sweeten the relationship by the day.

Communication includes things that are said as well as things that are not said. It includes what is inferred as well as what is implied. It is not only the words that are spoken, but also the way the words are spoken.

A hallmark of poor communication is when one spouse says to the other, "You should have known!" That statement is a recipe for failure, because you didn't marry a mind reader. Your spouse won't and should not be expected to know if you don't tell them. Talk and communicate with each other. Notice, we did not say just talk, we also said communicate with each other. Be open to non-verbal communication cues, as well. Body language can say a lot.

My friend, Steven Gaffney, who is a business communications expert and author of the book, *Honest Communication*, says that great organizations are built on open and honest communication, and that effective communication requires being able to get the unsaid said. This means getting people to open up and stop withholding information, because a problem cannot be resolved if it is withheld. This concept applies to marriages as well. Great marriages are built on open and honest communication. When spouses withhold information or choose not to discuss issues, it tears down trust and negatively impacts the marriage itself. Imagine a company had a really great employee but something happened and that employee left without telling the boss why. If the boss had known the reason, then he/she could have addressed it. The same is true for sharing information in your relationships.

Stonewalling

Withholding information can come in a number of ways. One way is when people only tell part of the truth. The trouble is that if your spouse only knows part of the story, it impacts the ability to get the whole issue resolved. Stonewalling is another way that information is withheld. According to the well-known marriage counselor, John Gottman, stonewalling is usually a male issue. It is when someone refuses to communicate and say things like, "This is the end of the conversation" or "Do whatever you want" or "No mas—I'm done." This can also sound like "I'm not talking to you!" Often this is a behavior that is taught to young men along with the concept of being strong, silent, and never crying. This is old fashion—and destructive—thinking.

Silent Treatment

Another form of withholding information is giving your spouse the silent treatment. This typically is a female way of not communicating. But shutting down all communication and hoping your spouse figures it out is not a wise way to keep the communication lines open. Though it isn't wise, it happens often in marriages. One of our friends shared that she would shut down and cut off all communication with her husband when she was angry, and her marriage ended in divorce. How can you communicate if you refuse to talk? The answer sounds obvious, but people behave this way all the time without considering what an absurd tactic it is, without thinking about the long-term impact.

Stamp Collecting

Another form of non-communicating is stamp collecting, which we mentioned in chapter three. Stamp collecting is when someone doesn't say what is bothering them at the moment it happens and holds it in. They continue to collect those situations without saying anything about how they feel or dealing with them as they occur. By keeping it inside, animosity builds up over time until it explodes. Eventually, a disagreement causes one spouse to bring up the whole stamp book of issues, and they spew everything out like a volcano.

The term stamp collecting is based on the concept of S&H Green Stamps. When I was a boy, we would go to the grocery store and when my mom got to the cashier and paid for the groceries, the cashier would take the money and give my mom a receipt along with some green stamps. Those green stamps were a reward for doing business with that store (similar to today's mileage rewards). My mom would take those stamps home and add them to a little book. When she filled all the spaces in the book with the appropriate number of stamps, she took them to a redemption center and traded the stamps for a gift. It might take ten books to get an AM/FM radio, twenty books to get a toaster, and thirty books to get a blender. You could get whatever you wanted. When you stamp collect in relationships, you hold on to the stamps to win an argument at a later time. There are many problems with stamp collecting, but one is that the other person often doesn't even remember the original issue because it was so long ago. This creates a mis-match, and it is not fair, nor is it the way to create a winning marriage.

The small issues that you keep to yourself are the ones that fester and eventually become major problems. We recommend you talk openly and honestly, so you can get it out. If you get it out, you can deal with it and resolve it so you can move on in a positive manner. Don't let the little molehills turn into major mountains!

Assumptions

When you have a problem and you are acting like you are not happy, but you don't tell your spouse what the problem is, then that person is left with one option, which is to make an assumption. When assumptions are made, you are getting into quicksand. This is a no-win position—it doesn't work for anyone. Effective relationships, whether personal or business, are not built on assumptions, but rather on open and honest communication.

While it is important to communicate honestly, it is also important that you share your concerns carefully and avoid being mean-spirited or hurtful. A major point of success in marriage is to communicate without purposely trying to hurt or get even with the other person. For God's sake, no muckraking.

Muckraking

Muckraking is like stamp collecting, but rather than concealing the stamps until there is an argument, muckraking brings up issues from the past, over and over again. Typically, those issues are past mistakes or failures that are used to gain an emotional advantage. This is a very destructive form of communication.

As a child, I remember being taught the phrase "Sticks and stones may break my bones, but words will never hurt me." Yet as I got older, I learned that words can hurt, and, worse, they can break our hearts. Mean, hurtful words can linger forever in your consciousness. Words can hijack your feelings and can keep you as a couple from being loving and intimate. When you are mean-spirited and hurtful in your attempts to win, you are actually losing. Hurtful and mean-spirited words cause loss of communication, loss of trust, and eventually the loss of your relationship. We recommend talking to each other with the goal of making things better. This mindset will allow you to talk with a positive purpose, or as Dee and I like to call it, "Sweet talk your spouse!"

Sweet Talk

We recommend you always communicate in a caring and loving way; you do that by thinking before you talk and keeping in mind that once a word is said, you can never take it back. Take some time and communicate with a goal of getting a positive result, not winning a personal victory. It is possible and doable. I attest that you can achieve this goal because I have personally experienced open, honest, and loving communication with Dee. As Dee and I say, "Learn to always sweet talk your spouse. Sweet always gets better results than sour."

I learned one of the best lessons on the importance of honest and loving communication from my Uncle Willie, who I am named after, and his wife, my Aunt Natla. They were together all the time, but I noticed they never seemed to argue and always were loving to each other. They made a point of always being pleasant in their communication, and they also made it a point to involve God in every decision. I was impressed by the way they consistently had a posture of thinking about what would be the Godly solution to their problem. Then how they discussed it in a pleasant way—no matter the circumstances.

Uncle Willie was one of the kindest men I ever met, so it's an honor to be named after him. Aunt Natla was a tough, no-nonsense person, who ran the family business. As tough as she was in business, she was always kind, loving, and pleasant to Uncle Willie They spoke sweetly to each other and communicated constantly. They talked about the business, their families, the community, and every topic in between.

They were a team, and they were in it to win it. But their idea of winning meant that God was involved in the winning and in the decision-making. From Uncle Willie and Aunt Natla,

I learned that integrity and communication were more than just words...integrity and communication is a lifestyle.

Integrity

For instance, when I was about seven years old, my mom took me and my brother, Noble, to spend a week with Uncle Willie and Aunt Natla. They lived in a rural part of Virginia called Keswick, and they owned a country store about a quarter mile from their home. Uncle Willie ran the store and Aunt Natla ran the home and the business's finances.

At the end of every day, Uncle Willie would bring us candy and bubble gum. And when we stopped by the store, he would often give us something to snack on and a soda pop to refresh us. One day, my brother and I walked to the store and asked Uncle Willie for some bubble gum. He had a long line of customers and told us he would bring some home for us later.

But my brother and I didn't want to wait. While Uncle Willie waited on the customers, we snuck behind the counter and took some bubble gum. We walked home chomping on our new bubble gum, and when we got home, Aunt Natla was waiting at the door.

She asked us how we enjoyed our time at the store and we said it was fine as we continued to chomp on our gum. She asked if we had seen Uncle Willie, and we said "Yes, but he was pretty busy." Then she asked, "You sure seem to be enjoying that gum. Where did you get that bubble gum?" We lied and said, "Ahh, Uncle Willie gave it to us."

Aunt Natla immediately picked up the phone, called the store, and asked Uncle Willie if he had given us any bubble gum. Uncle Willie responded that he'd been very busy and couldn't give us any bubble gum. Aunt Natla looked at us again and said, "Now, I know you boys didn't have any money, so where did you get the bubble gum?" We realized we were sunk, so we confessed. We had taken the bubble gum while Uncle Willie was busy helping customers.

Aunt Natla told us that we were not only thieves, but also liars. She said that men of integrity never stole and never lied. Aunt Natla said she was not only disappointed, but she was hurt by us taking something that they freely gave us when they had time. As we sat there, sucking up our tears, we wondered how in the world she knew that we had taken the bubble gum. For the life of us, we couldn't figure out how she knew. In time, I figured it out. They communicated about everything. While we thought we were being slick and stealing the bubble gum, Uncle Willie had seen it, and while we were walking home, he had called Aunt Natla. They talked often and talked about everything.

Uncle Willie arrived home that evening and sat us down and shared that his success was built on his commitment to integrity and honesty. He was disappointed in us, and said he hated to have to discipline us, but that was what we deserved. So, he gave us a spanking. A few days later, my mom returned to Keswick to pick us up. When she learned of our behavior, she expressed her disappointment and gave us a spanking as well.

This same scene was replayed again when we got home to Washington, D.C. Our dad told us he was disappointed in us; to discipline us he gave us demerits, which meant additional chores. About two weeks later, when we went to Philadelphia to visit our grandmother, she told us how disappointed she was and gave us a spanking as well!

You might think this was a lot of spanking and disciplining over a few pieces of bubble gum. Today, some people might say it was child abuse, but, in retrospect, I am so grateful for their discipline. Here' s the big picture lesson: From that day to this day I have never touched anything that did not belong to me. I've made it my mission to be a man of my word, and always do what I say. I promised Dee if she would live with me in my mother's attic for a year, I would buy her a house. And I kept my word! And I have tried to do the same with each and every promise I have made to her over the years.

The honesty lesson was not the only lesson I learned from that experience with Uncle Willie and Aunt Natla. There are two other major lessons I want to share with you from that story. One is that little problems should be handled while they are still small and before they develop into destructive issues. It started with two pieces of bubble gum, but it also stopped with those two pieces of bubble gum. I have never taken anything, small or big, since that day. The lesson is to keep the small things, small. Don't let them grow into big things.

The other lesson is about communication. Uncle Willie and Aunt Natla communicated and talked about everything. They worked together on everything—even on straightening out their nephews. Great marriages are built on great communication. Dee and I talk about everything! We talk about the good, the bad, and the uncomfortable. We talk about our ups and downs, our hurts and fears, and our pains. We even talk about topics that many people find too uncomfortable to discuss—like death. We talk about how we want our affairs handled when we die, and we have prepared our wills and shared them with each other. Death is inevitable, (I have yet to find anyone who gets out of this life alive). Everyone is going to leave here one day, yet many people refuse to talk about it.

Personal Space

Although Dee and I talk about everything, we are mindful that individuals need personal space, even in the midst of marriages. You probably don't like it when people invade your personal space and get too close when you're talking in public social settings. In the same way, we also understand that individuals in marriage need space, especially during intense personal conversations. We like the term our pastor, John K. Jenkins, Sr. uses, which is, "intense fellowship." This is his term for handling challenging discussions in a Godly way. Even people of faith can have intense fellowship. In those times, some people need space to calm down and get their thoughts together.

We recommend that if one person in the relationship asks for space, then you should give it to them. In fact, we recommend you develop some "pattern interrupt" techniques to use when you feel like you are about to lose your temper or say something that you will regret. Pattern interrupt is a way to stop the anger for a moment and get to a calm, clear thinking space. In my book *A Setback Is A Setup For A Comeback,* I explain that anger is the word danger without the letter d, and the d stands for discipline. You may need to count to ten, take a walk around the block, or breathe deeply until you calm down. Whatever technique you use, make it a part of your discipline when you feel yourself getting angry. When you and your spouse are in "intense fellowship" and your spouse needs a minute, give it to them.

Nagging

Nagging is another form of destructive communication. To nag means to bother someone with constant complaints or by constantly finding fault. There is an old saying that "nagging, like harping, should be left to musical instruments." One problem with nagging is that it actually shuts down communication. Dee and I were counseling a couple where the wife nagged the husband to the point that he would try to avoid talking to her. Even when the wife was pregnant and close to her due date, she called him on his cell phone and he looked at his phone, saw her name, and let it go to voicemail! When his friend chided him for not answering the call from his pregnant wife, he said, "She is just going to nag me!" Both the husband and wife were at fault in the scenario. The husband should have taken the wife's call, no matter what. And the wife had done such an effective job of conditioning her husband's behavior, by nagging, that she created a block to their communication. Nothing good is achieved by nagging, so don't do it.

Respect The Call

The person you married is also the one you chose, so make a point to speak to them with love and respect. We are all human, of course, and occasionally things might not be said with the appropriate tone of respect and love. It happens. When it does, be open to how the other person says that it makes them feel. For example, during pickup basketball games, when a person calls "foul," it is universally accepted that you must respect the call. So too, must you respect the call when your mate says their feelings have been hurt. It is important that you tell your spouse how their words made you feel. Remember that no one can tell you how you feel. Your spouse might not have intended for the words to have that impact, but only you can say how the words made you feel. Do what Dee and I do: share that pain quickly, talk it out, and then, just as quickly, apologize.

Fix Before Bedtime

Finally, when problematic issues arise, make it your standard operating policy that you will not take those issues to bed with you. Fix them before going to sleep. Believe it or not, this is a major point that came out in conversations with every long-term married couple we interviewed. Each said that they kiss and make up before going to bed. Every couple we interviewed, who were married over twenty-five years, mentioned this standard operating procedure as a key to their success in creating a happy marriage. Therefore, we suggest that you follow the lead of successful couples and never go to bed without having first solved the problem. Period.

SELLING IS GOOD FOR BUSINESS AND MARRIAGE

When I started in business, I learned it was important to sell my ideas, products, and services to potential clients. Since I've been married, I've learned that successfully married couples are able to sell their ideas to their spouses. When we first got married, I had to sell Dee on taking a vacation. It sounds strange, but it's true. Dee came from a family that never took a vacation. Her parents owned a grocery store, where they worked Monday through Saturday. Her father was a pastor and her mother was the First Lady and head deaconess of the church, so they were busy every Sunday with church activities. They loved what they did and they did it together, so they never took vacations. When Dee and I got married, she was not interested in us taking time and resources to vacation either.

On the other hand, I was from a family that traveled a lot. My mom loved to travel and we were on the road almost every weekend. We would travel to Philadelphia to visit my grandmother one weekend, and then travel to Virginia to visit her aunts and uncles the next weekend. On other weekends, we would go visit my father's sister in Baltimore. And since my mom was a school teacher and had her summers off, we were always on the go during the summer months. I was used to traveling and enjoyed going on vacations. When we got married, I was looking forward to traveling with Dee and taking nice vacations. But when I mentioned it to Dee, she was not feeling it. So, I had to sell her on it, and it took some work. Eventually I was able to convince her that it was good for our business to take a vacation. With a vacation, we could get renewed and re-energized for the entrepreneurial journey we were on. We went on our first vacation to St Martin, in the Caribbean. She loved it! Since then, we have scheduled vacations every year. Now she often is the one who plans the vacations and takes care of all the travel arrangements.

Dee sells me on things as well. When we first got married, I was not very neat. She is super neat; some would call her a neat freak. Dee likes to have everything orderly and in place. So rather than nag me to clean up, she sold me on keeping things neat and how much easier my life would be if I had things organized. Plus, she rewarded me for my efforts. I really liked the reward, and I was sold! From that day to this, I have been working on being neat and organized.

Sell your spouse by influencing them rather than nagging or browbeating them. Help them see your position and perspective, and sell them on how it could be in their interests to try your idea. Arguing never changes anyone's mind. It's like the old adage "A person convinced against their will is of the same opinion still!" If you are arguing, you are trying to force your spouse to go along with you. If you persuade them, you get them to come along with you of their own volition.

When you persuade your spouse, it becomes a win-win situation. Instead of arguing, we recommend you share a convincing story or example to get your spouse to understand your position. Then explain how your position could be of benefit to you both—and hopefully your spouse will see that and agree.

Here is the formula for selling your ideas:

1. **First, and foremost, no drama.**
2. **Take a deep breath.**
3. **Lower your voice.**
4. **Think positive and think win-win!**
5. **Be sweet! As one of my mentors said, "You can force your way through by hollering or getting loud—or by using honey. Honey is so much sweeter!"**
6. **Ask yourself what evidence you might use to convince your spouse to see it from a different perspective.**
7. **Tell your story.**
8. **Maintain respect in your conversations; even if you disagree, you can do so without being disagreeable.**

It is ironic that at this point in history, when we have so many modes of communication available, people have so much trouble communicating effectively. We recommend you make it a point to sometimes forgo the high-tech methods and use a high-touch method instead: talk to each other. Have an in-person, calm conversation with each other. Keep the conversation calm and respectful and work at seeing the issue from your spouse's perspective.

We especially recommend that you do not argue or have "intense fellowship" (a nice way to say argue) via email, text or social media. If you are in close proximity, we recommend you work through it in person; if that is not possible, then we recommend you pick up the phone and talk! High tech is great for speed but not for tone and inflection of voice. Sometimes it is not what you say as much as how you say it, that can make the big difference. Pick up the phone and talk to each other...

it can save a lot of misunderstanding and hurt feelings!

DEE'S PERSPECTIVE

It is not just what you say, but how you say it. The intent behind the words is just as important as the words we speak. Willie and I call it "sweet talk." Do you speak to your spouse as if they were precious cargo—marked fragile, handle with care? Sweet talk is the tone of voice and even the inflection you use when you converse with your spouse. It's communicating with respect and honor for your spouse.

My office manager brought something interesting to my attention about how I talk to Willie. One afternoon I was on the phone handling a high-stress business negotiation. The person on the other end of the phone was pushy, talking tough and trying to take advantage of my pleasant tone. I pushed back, because I was not going to be intimidated. While on hold during a break in our negotiations, Willie called on my cell, and when I spoke to him, she noticed that my tone was completely different. After completing the negotiation (where I was successful in getting what we were due), my office manager brought the tone difference to my attention. She said, "WOW! No wonder you two have such a great marriage. You actually talk to him sweetly, even in moments of stress!" We recommend you do the same with your spouse. God recommends sweet talk too:

- "Gracious words are a honeycomb, sweet to the soul and healing to the bones." (Proverbs 16:24; NKJV)
- "A gentle answer turns away wrath, but a harsh word stirs up anger." (Proverbs 15:1; NIV)

My father, Rev. Rivers S. Taylor, Sr., was a fire-and-brim-stone preacher in the pulpit. But once the collar and robe were removed, he always spoke gently and lovingly to his wife and family. My daddy never raised his voice to me, so I don't accept loud and rude behavior from anyone. It was one of the issues we had to work through early on in our marriage. Willie made a promise to never raise his voice to me, and he has kept his word.

My dad was the head of the household, but my parents' marriage was not a dictatorship but a terrific partnership. Dad ran the businesses and brought in the revenue, but mom ran the household and managed the administration and financials for the businesses. Dad made the final calls on the big issues, but he rarely had to make those calls because mom never let the little issues become big ones. On those few times when the issues were big enough to get to Dad, he would ask Mom for her thoughts before making a final decision.

In terms of how to handle the kids, Mom would often defer to Dad, and then he quickly deferred back to Mom. It was frustrating for us kids! It was impossible to get them to disagree—at least in front of us. There was no playing one against the other because they were always on the same page. There was no arguing or fussing; they just worked together like a well-oiled machine, and it was all supported by the way they talked to each other.

Pleasant, Tender Communication

When you are pleasant and tender in your communication, your mate is inclined to lean in and listen longer. Communication leads to understanding, and understanding leads to solutions. And sometimes those solutions are the result of a tremendous ability to find common ground and to compromise. With compromise we avoid criticism, defensiveness, contempt, and stonewalling, which, according to the Gottman Institute, are the "Four Horsemen" that lead to divorce. The Gottman Institute focuses on relationship research. Hopefully by recognizing the Four Horsemen, you can stop them in their tracks. They are:

1. **Criticism**— pointing out the faults in your spouse and acting as if you have none.
2. **Defensiveness**— being extremely sensitive to criticism and responding in a hostile manner.
3. **Contempt**—having an open and obvious lack of respect for your spouse.
4. **Stonewalling**—refusing to communicate and cooperate with your spouse and shutting down.

We add muckraking and stamp collecting to Gottman's list of situations to avoid which will keep you from destroying your marriages. Focus instead on principles that can grow your relationships. One of those key principles is the importance of compromise.

Compromise

Successful marriages know the value of compromise, and use it often. Compromise can be achieved through consistent communication. To get to compromise, we each must be willing to share why we think and feel a certain way on an issue while the other person listens intently. The next step is for the listener to summarize and repeat back what they believe you've said, and ask, "Is that what you're saying? Is that what you meant?" Listen and repeat until there is true understanding. This process is called L.Q.C. (Listen, Question, Clarify). Without effective communication and clarity, assumptions are made, and assumptions don't promote genuine understanding.

The more you communicate, the better you will become at it. Willie and I have worked hard over the years on our communication skills. What we have learned is that one partner need not dominate the conversation in order for both parties to express themselves. Some individuals tend to be more talkative and outgoing than others. But that doesn't mean that the quieter partner is shut out. An example of this tactic was pointed out to us after Willie and I had lunch with a young couple to share our marriage secrets. What they found most helpful was how Willie and I stopped talking when the other one had something to say. Willie would be talking, and I would get an idea and interject, and Willie would stop. Then other times, Willie would interject, and I would stop talking. We never talked over each other or tried to have the last word. We worked together and communicated, like a tag team. The young couple said if they tried to do that, there would be a World War III due to talking over each other! We shared that we learned to be a "yin and yang of communication," like one person with two mouths, interjecting as the spirit gives utterance. That skill takes time, patience, and understanding of one's spouse, but it is possible and quite beautiful to experience.

In time, you can communicate without saying a word. Often, Willie and I will simply look at each other and know exactly what the other is thinking or getting ready to do. There are times when he finishes my sentences and vice versa. This comes from practice, so begin working on this today and before you know it, you'll be in beautiful unison.

THE POWER OF ACTIVE AND EFFECTIVE LISTENING

A critical part of being a good communicator is being a good listener. Certainly, if you want to live in harmony as a married couple, it is crucial that you slow down, close your mouth, and take time to listen to your spouse.

Active listening is when you are fully focused on someone's

words and tone while they are talking. The evidence is that you are nodding to indicate understanding or asking a question for clarity. This shows you are absorbing what your mate is saying. You are focused on their ideas, not just waiting for your turn to talk!

Try this: when your spouse has completed expressing themselves, summarize what you believe you heard them say, and ask if you got the information accurately. Next, deliver your response in a thoughtful manner that does not demean your spouse's viewpoint.

We recommend you talk to each other and not at each other! Talking to each other is to talk a bit and then listen to get the other person's feelings and perspective. To talk at someone is to talk and talk and talk, never stopping to listen to the other person's thoughts and feelings. Sometimes this is called "Talking Over" the other person. Talking at someone also includes discounting their feelings and not giving their ideas any validity.

Research shows that by listening actively, you get a clearer understanding of what is important to your spouse, increasing trust between the two of you and helping to minimize conflict. God gave us two ears and one mouth for a reason. Therefore, we must work to listen twice as much as we speak.

On a speaking tour to Australia, Willie shared the stage with Dr. Stephen Covey, the author of the landmark book *The 7 Habits of Highly Effective People*. One of the key tenets of his book is the importance of listening for active and effective communication. Dr. Covey wrote, "Seek first to understand, THEN seek to be understood." Seek first not to speak, but seek to hear what your spouse is saying, and then, once you have understood their point of view, you can share your ideas.

By being an active (and thus, effective) listener and gently asking probing questions to follow up, you can learn what to say and how to say it in a way that will be well received by your spouse. Active and effective listening may seem like small issues and may not sound very interesting or important, but can have a large positive impact on your marriage and your level of intimacy.

♥ JOLLEY ADVICE

1. **Develop your listening skills.** Ask questions and then be quiet while your spouse gets their chance to speak. Listen more than you speak.

2. **Study your spouse.** Learn the meaning of their body language as well as the inflections in their voice.

3. **Respect each other's communication style.** Identify your spouse's communication style, and discern the differences that reflect their emotions—from being under stress to expressing pleasure. Know how to adapt and adjust your communication accordingly.

4. **It's not just what you say, but how you say it.** Agree on the tone of voice you two will use to communicate with each other. Honor and respect that agreement, especially when you disagree.

5. **Create a safe place to communicate.** Make your relationship a safe place to share disappointments and sorrows. Be a source of comfort and safety. Be a haven for sharing sensitive information.

6. **Never talk over each other.** Work on creating a "yin and yang communication" style. No one person should dominate the conversation. Take turns talking, and remember that you should listen to each other more than you talk.

7. **Be open and honest in your conversations.** Say what you have to say, with love and care, and make a point to not withhold anything. Don't allow any stamp collecting or muckraking in your marriage.

8. **Remember you are not married to a mind reader!** If you want your spouse to know what you are feeling or thinking, tell them and never assume they should know.

9. **Use sweet talk to get the information to your spouse.** Your spouse will pay better attention, meaning the information will be more accurately conveyed, and, ultimately, your intimacy will be deepened.

♥

CHAPTER FIVE

Leave the Drama with Your Mama!

"There is a psychological law that says:
Focus on peace and you prosper; focus on drama and you flounder."
~ Dr. David Goodman

Dee and I highly recommend that when you marry, you leave the drama with your mama! Our friend, Dr. Clarice Fluitt, a tremendous speaker, author, and minister has been married to her husband George, for over fifty years. Over the years, she has counseled countless couples and seen all kinds of drama. Dr. Clarice often says: "Love is blind, but marriage is an eye opener!" We agree with Dr. Clarice and recommend you make your marriage no reality show spectacle!

WILLIE'S PERSPECTIVE

Dee and I define drama as negative and "messy" situations that create anxiety and stress in the lives of the people it's directed towards. This includes behavior such as hollering, screaming, nagging, temper tantrums, shutting down communication, and pre-planned emotional exhibitions, like fake crying. During reality television shows, increased drama brings higher ratings. But, marriages built on drama will only result in low ratings on the home front and the unraveling of your marriage.

There are so many "real housewives" shows on television that we might be persuaded to believe that those housewives are behaving the way you should handle your marriage relationships. Nothing could be further from the truth! Their lives and their marriages are scripted and designed to be filled with drama and craziness to keep viewers watching, keep people talking about it, and getting even more people to watch. That is not the lifestyle you should model in your marriage. "Drama" is never conducive to a long-term, happy marriage.

Leave, Cleave, Weave

Your home should always be a place of peace, safety, and happiness. To make your home your sanctuary, you both must make the decision to ditch the drama and leave it at your parents' house. You should "leave, cleave, and weave." What does that mean? Genesis 2:24 says, "That is why a man leaves his father and mother and is united to his wife, and they become one flesh" (NIV). When you marry, you leave the parent/child relationship and create a new family. Then you cleave to your mate, which means to bond and become one with your spouse. Then you weave a new life together. Scripture also says, "When I was a child, I talked like a child, I thought like a child, I reasoned like a child. When I became a man, I put the ways of childhood behind me" (1 Corinthians 13:11; NIV). We recommend that when you get married you leave childish behaviors in your past.

When I was a child, I had terrible temper tantrums; I stomped my feet and hollered and screamed to try and get my way. It didn't work! As I grew older, I realized those behaviors did not serve me well, and the tantrums never got me what I wanted. Instead, they created more problems than they solved, so I changed and learned to control my temper and the drama. The same applies in marriage. When you marry and leave home, you will discover some of your childish actions will not serve you well, so you will need to change in order for your relationship to thrive.

Drama

If you are still dating, we recommend you watch for the drama signs early, and realize that if you see drama early in your relationship, you will probably see it again. There are numerous verses in Proverbs that talk about the drama of a contentious spouse and how difficult it can be to live in the same house. Proverbs 21:9 says, "It is better to live in a corner of a roof than in a house shared with a contentious spouse" (NASB). And Proverbs 27:15 says, "A nagging spouse is like the drip, drip, drip of a leaky faucet; You can't turn it off, and you can't get away from it" (MSG). Yet Proverbs also talks about how great it is to have a wonderful mate. Proverbs 31:10–11 says, "A good woman is hard to find, and worth far more than diamonds. Her husband trusts her without reserve, and never has reason to regret it" (MSG).

Just to be clear, both husbands and wives can create drama. Most people talk about drama queens, but there can be drama kings as well. We know, because we've met them. We once counseled a couple where the husband was the drama king. The wife was a high-energy, perky person and the husband was usually a quiet, easygoing guy—that is, until they argued. During disagreements, the husband would become the drama king and say mean-spirited things to the wife that would break her spirit and make her quiet and sad. The husband came from a family that used drama to get what they wanted, so this was business as usual for him. To make matters worse, he knew his wife's weak spot, which made her unable to compete in disagreements. She suffered from severe separation anxiety, because her father had left the family when she was a child and this haunted her into adulthood. Consequently, the easygoing husband would use his knowledge of his wife's weakness to get his way by threatening to leave her whenever they disagreed. In response, she would fall apart.

When we met with them, the wife articulated her anxiety issues. We shared with them how destructive drama could be, and worked with them to set new rules on how they would handle disagreements. They both promised to abide by these new rules. A few months later, I got a call from the husband. He said he had messed up. They had a disagreement, and he had immediately reverted to his drama tactics. Her response was, "You promised, and you broke your promise!" He asked me to intervene, but I told him I would not, because he had broken his promise to her and to us. I told him I was disappointed that he would bring back the drama tactics when he promised he would not. Eventually, I spoke to the wife and she said that he had broken his promise and she could no longer trust him. I recommended they get crisis marriage counseling, but she said she was done. She went on to file for divorce. We asked her to reconsider and she said no. We continue to pray for them, yet we realize this situation would never have occurred if he had simply kept his promise and left the drama with his mama or with the family environment where he grew up.

DRAMA ANTIDOTE #1:
MAKE YOUR SIGNIFICANT OTHER FEEL SIGNIFICANT

One of the secrets to a successful relationship is to make your spouse feel significant, as often as you can. Make them feel special and important. I have been doing this for years, and I know it works. I am often asked about the recognition I give Dee in my programs. I talk about her in every speech. When

I initially mention her, I stop and tell the audience, "Please excuse me, but when I mention my bride, I get weak in my knees. I get weak because we are newlyweds, and I really am smitten by her." Then I say, "Yes, we're newlyweds. We have been married for over thirty years. People always ask how do I say I'm a newlywed after over thirty years in a marriage? My answer is that I still have the fire for her; I would crawl over broken glass to get to her; and I have told her on numerous occasions that if she leaves me, I'm coming with her!" After people finish laughing, I share that this is one of the reasons why we have been able to stay married for so long. I believe one of the reasons we are happily married is that we both make a concerted effort to make the other feel special every opportunity we can. Dee doesn't speak as often as I do, but she makes me feel special every day. Sometimes it is the things she does for me to help me with my goals and dreams, and sometimes it is just by the way she says hello. It really is the little things, that mean so much. This sentiment has been captured in my song, "Little Things!" (The full song lyrics are available at the end of the book.)

Men often ask me, "How do I make my wife feel special?" First, I suggest keeping your relationship top of mind. For example, when you wake in the morning, say, "I love you." Secondly, be thoughtful. Do little things that your wife enjoys, such as preparing her favorite snack and delivering it to her, just because you can. These small gestures work for husbands and for wives, and they do not take a lot of extra work. They literally just take moments of your day to make your spouse feel better and let them know you think they are awesome. But even if it does take extra work and time, it is always worth it. I have learned that if you treat her like a queen, she will treat you like a king.

DRAMA ANTIDOTE #2:
SPEAK WELL OF YOUR SPOUSE IN PUBLIC AND IN PRIVATE

Your words have power. I strongly believe in the power of our words to shape our lives. If you say you are sick, you will be sick. If you say you are poor, you will be poor. If you say your children are bad, they will be terrible. And if you say I love you often, it will have a positive impact on your relationship. Say "I love you" every day, because the more you say it, the more it becomes your reality.

The more you tell yourself that you love your spouse, the less your mind will be open to stupid thoughts and, then, stupid actions. Marriages can be drastically altered and damaged by the stupid thoughts that create stupid actions. And never make jokes or negative statements about your marriage. Don't be like the guy I met who jokingly said, "This is my future ex-wife." Not long after that, she was!

DRAMA ANTIDOTE #3:
BE CONSIDERATE

"If you want to stay happily married, you must learn to be considerate of your mate. You must think about your spouse as you think about yourself," said marriage veteran Herman Thompson. Herman and his wife Claudia have been married for over fifty years. They shared a story with us about being considerate that happened when they first married and has helped them to stay married.

Herman said his mother was known as a great cook. All his siblings and many of his friends made it a practice to stop by in the evenings to taste her culinary creations. When Herman was newly married, he stopped by his mother's house after work to check on her. All of his siblings and many of his friends were already there, in great anticipation of his mother's dinner for that evening.

When Herman pulled up a chair, his mother said, "No! You do not eat without your wife being here. You are married now. You need to go home and see if your wife has cooked dinner. If she has, you eat what she cooked. If she has not cooked, then you bring her back here and the two of you eat together! Now that you are married you must think about her and her feelings as much as you think about you and yours." From that day on, Herman honored his mother's lesson and always thought of his wife, as he thought about himself. He said that was one of the best lessons he learned to help him establish a successful marriage that has lasted over fifty years.

DRAMA ANTIDOTE #4:
FORGIVENESS

Humans are flawed and make mistakes. Not some people—but everyone. That is why forgiveness is so important in a marriage. Sooner or later one of you will do something, say something, or neglect to do something that will hurt your spouse's feelings. At that time, I recommend that you sincerely apologize. And when your spouse apologizes for something, it is very important to accept the apology and move on, which demonstrates what forgiveness really is.

I learned about forgiveness from my wife and the way she handled a mistake I made due to poor judgment. We were scheduled to leave for an evening flight to Greensboro, North Caroline, for an event there the next morning. Our flight departed from Washington Reagan airport at 7 p.m., and Dee started asking me about leaving for the airport around 3:30 p.m., because she hates being late and rushing. I on the other hand, love getting to the airport about thirty minutes before the cut-off time. She continued to ask if I was ready to go because she felt we needed extra time due to rush hour. I reminded her that I was the seasoned traveler, and I had it all together. I had calculated the travel time and the traffic, and I knew the perfect time to leave home. I reminded her of previous flights where we had arrived so early that we had to sit around and wait for a long time. I told her we would be there in more than enough time.

Finally, I told her it was time to leave, and we left ... and proceeded to get caught in the worst traffic I have ever seen! Of course, we missed the cut-off time for the flight. Although I told the airline agent about the traffic and how important it was for me to be on that flight because I had an event the next morning, she was not impressed. She shook her head and said our seats had been given away! As I continued to plead my case, Dee just stood by my side and didn't say a word. Finally, the airline agent was able to get us a connecting flight through Philadelphia that would get us there before morning, but it would be a long slog and a long layover.

Dee never said a word. She didn't have to because I already knew I had messed up! She could have said, "I told you so," but she didn't, and I appreciated that because I was already beating myself up, and didn't need any cheerleaders joining in. I apologized to her and told her she was right, and she quickly said, "I forgive you. We are in this together!" Needless to say, since then I have listened to her counsel about travel times. The lesson here is three-fold: 1. Be willing to apologize when you mess up. 2. The spouse should accept the apology quickly, and move on. 3. There's no need to say, "I told you so!" That never makes the situation better.

Be mindful that some people simply like drama. They actually enjoy it. If you are not yet married, choose wisely. If you see drama early in your relationship, you will probably see it again. Maya Angelou said it best, "When someone shows you who they are, believe them the first time!"

DEE'S PERSPECTIVE

Drama is a choice. Once you understand that, you realize drama is never necessary. An example of this was the time I had dinner with my first husband and my last husband —Willie. That's right, both husbands at the same time! Both were sitting right across from me in a booth we shared at a busy restaurant.

It was Howard University's annual homecoming weekend, which attracts thousands of alums. Willie and my former husband were engrossed in pleasant conversation. You would have thought they were old college friends. No drama. How did this come to be?

It started years earlier, when our home phone rang. Willie answered, and the voice on the other end said it was my former husband. He was in town and on his way to visit his sister-in-law. He thought he was near our home and asked if he could stop by and say hello. Willie said, "Absolutely, come on by!"

When he got there, Willie said I was out running errands but would be back soon. Willie offered him a soft drink while he waited. My former husband had never met my son William, who was at Howard's law school at the time. Willie called William and asked him to come home to meet mom's first husband. William came from studying and greeted my former husband with a big smile and a handshake. By the time I got home, the three men were having a lively chat, like old friends. When I walked in my ex said he was blown away by the graciousness of Willie and William. "You guys are so kind to me," he said.

"I feel welcomed in your home." Willie assured him that he was welcome anytime. He shared that we don't have drama because it's not productive, so he need not worry.

When he arrived in D.C. for homecoming weekend, he called and invited us to meet him at the host hotel for dinner. We had a pleasant evening together. There was no drama, because we understand that drama does not provide the kind of life we want to create for ourselves.

Drama-free living must extend to all aspects of our lives. Willie and I were invited and attended the wedding of his daughter's mother. Not only did we attend, but Willie participated in the ceremony! We could all celebrate their happy occasion because Willie and I had worked very hard to develop a positive, cooperative, respectful relationship with her over the years.

When we share these experiences with others, many are amazed at how we are able to make all of this work. The answer is we decided! We decided we would have a marriage that was drama free. It takes constant open and honest communication; being willing to listen, and always working through the challenges, and it is always worth the effort.

The Bible tells us, "If possible, so far as it depends on you, live peaceably with all" (Romans 12:18; ESV) And Ephesians 4:29 says, "Let no corrupt communication come out of your mouths, but only such as is good for building up, as fits the occasion, that it may give grace to those who hear" (ESV). In other words, operate with the mindset of getting along with people—leave the drama with your mama!

♥ JOLLEY ADVICE

1. **Drama and crazy is a choice.** As things get crazy in life, don't get crazy with them. Be gracious and make peace. It works if you work it.
2. **It takes two.** Accept responsibility for your part and do all you can to make it right.
3. **Be kind and continue to extend an olive branch.** When things go in the wrong direction, be wise enough to apologize so drama doesn't get a foothold. You'll feel better about yourself.
4. **Always be considerate.** Practice always thinking about your mate and how they feel.
5. **Make your home a no-drama zone.** Decide to have a drama-free marriage, and then carry that out with your commitment.
6. **Stay away from drama queens and kings.** Decide to hang with positive, upbeat people. You will become like the people you spend time with, either good or bad.
7. **When you see drama early in a prospective spouse, don't think you will change them by marrying them.** When people show you who they are, believe them the first time!

CHAPTER SIX

Agree about Disagreeing

"In every disagreement in marriage,
remember this one important truth-
my spouse is my partner not my enemy.
We will either win together or we will lose together."
~ Dave Willis

WILLIE'S PERSPECTIVE

In every relationship, you will have times when you won't
agree. Those are delicate times when relationships can be hurt,
and, if not handled well, they can even be broken. This is why
it's wise to decide ahead of time on the rules of engagement
regarding how you will handle those moments when you disagree.

As two individuals coming together to create one couple,
there is a good chance that the two of you will eventually
disagree about something. We recommend you talk about
how you will disagree in advance. It may sound strange to
talk about disagreements before they even happen, but if you
plan out how to handle disagreements before they occur, you
have a better chance of finding common ground during those
challenging times. You can even respectfully agree to disagree!

Rules of Engagement

We have discovered it is better to set boundaries on the front end than to try and fix a broken relationship on the back end. To do this, we recommend you sit down with your spouse and discuss what you both deem to be fighting fair. Now, to be clear, we use the word fight figuratively. When you don't fight fair, you might win the small battle, but you will lose the real victory—being happily married! The things you want to discuss are the acceptable and unacceptable words and behaviors during a disagreement, and what items are "below the belt" (for example, talking about his mama or her family).

When you are deciding on your rules of engagement, you should each put an equal number of issues on the table. If the husband has two issues, so should the wife, and vice versa. Talk about how the below-the-belt issue (or issues) makes you feel, and why it's important to you. The other person must listen with empathy and not become defensive. It's important to keep in mind that you can never dispute the feelings of another person. You might not agree, but these are still their feelings. Therefore, you must respect their feelings and then honor them by enacting new behaviors based on the rules you each have agreed to. You might not agree with the way your spouse feels, but you have to respect the feelings of that individual; respect how they say the disagreement made them feel. Once you agree on a system, you must honor the agreement.

We can honestly say that by practicing this behavior, we have not had an argument in over thirty years. Once we established our rules of engagement, we never crossed each other's lines. But it was not always this way. In fact, our first big argument was almost the end of our marriage, and it happened because of Chinese food.

Here's what happened. Dee and I had been married a few months and her brother and his wife were coming to visit. We decided to get Chinese takeout for dinner and stopped at a restaurant in D.C.'s Chinatown neighborhood. It had been one of my favorite places to get food when I was single. I knew their menu well, so I picked out four dishes I thought would be good for dinner. Dee said that we needed to order more dishes, but I told her four large dishes from this restaurant would be more than enough for six people. She said she didn't want to run out of food and be embarrassed. I assured her that this restaurant was known for its large portions, and I expressed to her again that four large dishes would be more than enough. However, she was not persuaded and insisted that we order more. I told her we would waste food and, worse, waste money if we ordered more.

We went back and forth on this issue, and the argument got more and more intense. I got louder and she got more insistent. It continued until I was hollering. Once I started hollering, she put her finger in my face and said, "I will not have you, or anyone else, hollering at me! My daddy never raised his voice to me, my brother never hollered at me, and neither will you! I WILL LEAVE YOU!"

Dial It Back

In that moment, I realized we were on our way to a bad ending and potentially a broken marriage. We had to stop and regroup. I took a breath and told Dee we needed to dial it back and get some clarity on this situation. We realized we were both out of control and needed to calm ourselves so we could get this situation settled. We didn't just need to settle the amount of food we should order, but, more importantly, we needed to develop a system for handling disagreements in our marriage.

I decided to purchase whatever she wanted; then we went home and had a family dinner with her brother, his wife and the rest of our family. That evening, when we were alone, we talked about what had happened, and how we could keep it from ever happening again. Dee said she could not accept anyone hollering at her, especially her husband, and I said I could not stand her threatening to leave me.

Rules of Engagement

We came up with some simple guidelines for how we would handle our disagreements. We call them our "rules of engagement." I promised I would not raise my voice when we disagreed, and she promised she would never threaten to leave me. Plus, we agreed to always be respectful of each other, especially when we are working through our differences of opinion. We made that agreement that night, and we've kept that promise. As a result, we have not had an argument in over thirty years.

Please do not think this means we have not disagreed with each other. We have disagreed about many things, but we have a system in place that allows us to come to an agreement without arguing.

One of the primary ways we avoid arguments is by never breaking the promise to abide by the agreement. You must keep your word! Earlier we shared the story of a couple with marital problems. The wife had separation anxiety issues, because her father had left the family when she was a child. During disagreements, the husband would threaten to leave, because he knew this was her weak spot.

Over dinner he promised to never do that again. He broke his promise, and they ended up divorced.

I share this story again because it contrasts with our story. Dee and I agreed on the rules of engagement and made a commitment to never, ever renege on that commitment. We've kept our promises to each other for over thirty years, and we have been able to stay happily married.

Our friend, John Morgan (the number-one George W. Bush impersonator, who toured with us on the Get Motivated Tour), says he and his wife Kathy have a unique system for solving problems. The foundation of their system is that they don't attack each other, rather they attack the problem together. Each problem that they face, they visualize throwing it on the other side of an imaginary net. Once the problem is on the other side of the net; the problem becomes the opponent (rather than each other). With this approach, they work on solving the problem, not fighting each other. Try this approach in deciding to work as a team, even on items you disagree on. You will experience more peace and happiness.

Settle Issues Before Bed

Another major recommendation we discussed earlier applies here as well. It is so important we are stating it again here, for emphasis. Each and every couple we interviewed insisted that it is critical to settle all issues before going to sleep. In other words, do not take today's problems with you into tomorrow. The Bible expresses this as well: "Do not let the sun go down while you are still angry" (Ephesians 4:26b; NIV). We implore you to follow that advice and resolve any problem before you go to bed.

DEE'S PERSPECTIVE

Our Chinese food carryout experience at the start of our marriage was all that was needed to get my attention. It made me more than willing to find a strategy on how to handle the disagreements that would come up in our marriage. What we developed has worked well in our business relationship as well.

"We should order these four dishes" said Willie, as we stood at the takeout counter in Chinatown. But I suggested more dishes than he thought we needed. I thought ordering an array of Chinese dishes would show my brother and his wife, who were visiting from Hampton, Virginia, that we were doing well. I wanted to impress them. I had no idea how many people each dish would feed and I never even thought to ask Willie. On top of that, I never ate Chinese food! I went straight to – "my way, or the highway!" As Willie disagreed, he got louder and I got angrier. He got louder and louder, and I got angrier and angrier. Eventually I said, "I don't like anyone hollering at me! I will leave you!" Willie was stunned and looked sad, and said he was sorry for hollering. At that point, I realized I had hurt his feelings and I apologized for threatening to leave him. Thankfully, we were able to dial it back, calm down, and then talk about it later that evening. That's when we decided we needed some rules on how we should disagree.

We have learned not to make mountains out of molehills. We learned to be slow to respond to a perceived offense. We had a discussion with a couple who had a big argument about who would turn off the lights when they left the house! Their argument was not really about the lights, but about their egos: Who was going to be in charge and make the final decision about the lights before leaving home? There's a great deal to argue about if you're going to argue about every little thing.

We have since learned that we achieve more together, plus we each get more of what we want when we honor the rules of engagement that we agreed to early on in our marriage.

Being on the same side of the table with my husband, whispering in his ear, sweet talking him, and advising him is better than hollering any day. Remember what Proverbs 19:10 says: "Good sense makes one slow to anger, and it is his glory to overlook an offense" (ESV).

♥ JOLLEY ADVICE

1. **Choose not to see every little thing as a problem.**
2. **Dial it back.** If you have a disagreement and you feel it is getting out of control, make a conscious decision to breathe, dial back your emotions, and talk calmly.
3. **Be quick to forgive, forget, and move on.** Apologize quickly and forgive quickly. Once the item is settled, move on and let it go.
4. **Work at creating win-win outcomes from challenging situations.** In his landmark book *The 7 Habits of Highly Effective People,* Dr. Stephen Covey said that the most effective people always seek win-win situations. The same is true for those in happy long-lasting marriages. Win-win solutions allow both partners to feel important, fulfilled, and happy.
5. **If you still find a point of disagreement, here is what we recommend:**
   - Review the points you have already agreed upon that are below the belt.
   - Ask this question before you say or do anything: What is more important, this issue or our relationship?
   - Ask your spouse why they feel the way they feel. Listen to their response. Restate the issue, asking them if your restatement is what they are communicating as the key issue or problem. Work to seek alternative solutions.
6. **Compromise.** Keep this in mind and repeat it to yourself over and over again: Happy spouse, happy house!

CHAPTER SEVEN

♥

How to Handle a Stalemate

"Yes, I depend on a man. He is the king of the house...
and I am the queen. We are a team. He depends on me and
I depend on him and that is how marriage is supposed to work."
~ Tammy Sousa

WILLIE'S PERSPECTIVE

As much as we have talked about how to disagree without being disagreeable, there may be times in your marriage when you have stalemates. Stalemates occur when the two of you come to a fork in the road and each of you have a different opinion on which way to go, and you are strongly committed to your position. Compromise seems impossible, and there is no consensus to be found. How do you come to a solution? Which way do you eventually go? These are the times when wisdom must come into play.

Webster's dictionary defines wisdom like this: a wise attitude, belief, or course of action; ability to discern inner qualities and relationships; good sense. The Bible states that wisdom is the "primary thing" and it also says, "Blessed are those who find wisdom, those who gain understanding, for she is more profitable than silver and yields better returns than gold. She is more precious than rubies; nothing you desire can compare with her" (Proverbs 3:13–15; NIV) I believe wisdom is not only good sense, it is also good sensing. This means to be open to look at the problem beyond ego and be open to wise counsel and Godly direction.

BECOME THE TRUSTED ADVISOR

Wisdom has shown us that Dee and I are partners in the success of our marriage. Therefore, we focus on the most positive result we can achieve with every situation. That has led us to use a concept called "trusted advisor" when it comes to stalemates. Even though we might not agree on a certain issue, we have developed a confidence in the advice of each other. If we disagree, I will ask her for more information on her position and she will do the same for me. We believe there might be a perspective we have not seen that would be helpful in making a final decision.

One of the examples we share about deciding which way to go when we have differing opinions is what we call the "go left or go right" analogy. Imagine that you are in the backseat of our car as Dee and I ride down a city street. As we get to a major intersection, I want to go left and Dee says she wants to go right. I say I really want to go left and she says she really wants to go right. I insist that left is the way to go and she insists that right is the way to go. Which way do we finally go?

Dee and I have figured out that the wisest thing to do is to consider the input of your trusted advisor, who is there to help you win. Therefore, I've learned to ask Dee why she wants to go right. I listen to her perspective. Over the years, I have chosen her way nine times out of ten. The reason I've chosen her way is that she is my trusted advisor, and I know that we are partners in this marriage and are trying to get to a positive solution.

It reminds me of when I was a little boy, and my mom and dad were in the front seat of the car and my brother and I were in the back seat. Dad would be driving and would want to change lanes. He would ask my mother for her opinion. This was before cars installed mirrors on the passenger side and he only had the top rear-view mirror to gauge the traffic situation. He knew there was a blind spot in his view of the traffic, so he asked his trusted advisor for her perspective. Mom would lean forward, roll down the window, stick her head partially out the window and let him know if he could change lanes or not. She was his trusted advisor and he depended on her advice. They were on the same team, with the same goal of safely reaching their destination together. Dee is my trusted advisor. We have learned to listen to each other and take each other's viewpoint into account before making pivotal decisions.

I bet you're wondering about the other time, the one out of ten times, when I really feel that I cannot go her way. We worked that situation out early in our marriage. We made a decision on who should break the tie. We used the Bible and Godly wisdom to help us make that decision. The Bible says that a husband should be the head of the household, and I hold that responsibility very seriously. Yet I know that head of the household does not mean a dictator, but rather a tie-breaker after wisely reviewing the situation with my best advisor, my wife.

VETO POWER

When I really think we should go left; have reviewed her perspective; but still think it is the best direction for us to take, I make the call to do so because as head of the household, that is my responsibility. Dee and I call it "veto power."

That's the power to break a tie. I asked for this when we first became husband and wife, and the reason I asked is that I knew I would need her buy-in for all decisions for long-term success. I never wanted Dee to feel like I was forcing her to do something. Instead, I promised that if she agreed to give me veto power, I would never abuse it. I have kept my promise. As our friends, B Smith and her husband Dan Gasby said, when I interviewed them on my Sirius XM Show, "It is not about ego, it is about how we go."

This veto power was tested early in our marriage. Typically, it was used in decisions involving our children, and we developed the tie-breaker philosophy because we were forced to. As discussed earlier, when we got married, we became a blended family. I was a single dad with a young daughter, Sherry, who lived with her mom but would come to stay with me over the summer. When she was with me, her good-time, fun-loving dad, her days were filled with dance lessons, summer camps, academic studies, and vacation Bible school camps. The rest of the time she would hang out with me and my music buddies. This involved taking her to gigs, jam sessions, recording studio sessions, rehearsals, and other kinds of musician stuff until the wee hours of the morning. No rules, lots of junk food, and certainly no set bedtime.

Then Dee and I got married, and Sherry came to live with us full-time, which, of course, included the school year. I was not prepared, in any sense of the word. We established routines for homework, chores, school uniforms, and bedtime. There was a lot going on and many new decisions to be made. New family structures were being established. It was no longer just fun and games. I had to have more focus, and Sherry had to become used to new routines and a life with a new woman in the household. When William, our second child, was born, things became even more complicated. In addition to the change in routine, Sherry had to get used to sharing me with others, because she was used to having me to herself.

Things became more complicated as Sherry grew into her teenage years. She wanted to date and I was not for it, and Dee agreed with me. She would call and complain to her mother that we were too strict and too fuddy-duddy. Her mother was more liberal, and told me that I should let her date at fifteen. I told her that was not going to happen. I had heard too many horror stories of young girls who got into trouble because they were allowed to make dating decisions long before they were ready. Plus, I knew how I had been when I was a young male! If Sherry was going to go out with boys, it would need to be supervised. Sherry and her mom did not like this, but Dee and I were on the same page and made the decision for our household. We were not going to be browbeaten into changing it.

We had gotten Sherry into the number-one academic high school in the city, and we had a routine in place to keep her moving toward getting into a good college. We also had a daily schedule of after-school enrichment activities for her, with a pickup and drop-off schedule that Dee and I coordinated. Since Dee worked downtown on Capitol Hill, she would drop the kids off on her way to work and pick them up on her way home. She would then drop Sherry off at her dance lessons and I would pick her up. One day in October, Dee called and said she was waiting outside of the school for Sherry, but Sherry was not there. She asked me if I had picked her up. I told her I had not. Dee went into the principal's office and was told that a woman had come from North Carolina with papers showing that she was Sherry's mother and had picked her up earlier that day to visit with her.

That evening, Sherry did not come home. Instead, we learned that her mother had taken her back to North Carolina. They had been planning it for weeks and we learned all the details when her mother called later that night. Her mother said Sherry did not like the fact that we would not let her go out on dates, nor that she had to finish her homework before watching TV in the evenings. Additionally, she did not like that we made her do her chores on the weekend before hanging out with her friends. All in all, my daughter said our approach to school and discipline was too demanding. Sherry was fed up with us and decided to escape to her mother's.

We were shocked, but her mother still had legal custody. We told her this was a mistake, but we would keep them in our prayers. We didn't like it, but we decided to move forward as a smaller unit, which we found to be easier and less stressful. Gone were the confrontations about homework, length of skirts, completing Saturday chores, dating, or any of the other issues we had grown accustomed to dealing with on a daily basis.

A few months later we got a call from Sherry's mother. We were in the midst of enjoying a quiet evening at home. Our son, William, four years old at the time, was sound asleep. Dee and her friend Darlene were chatting, and I was reading, when the phone rang. On the other end of the line, I heard Sherry's mother's voice hollering, "Please come get this girl! She is driving me crazy!!! She won't do anything I ask. She is disrespectful and rude to me. Plus, she's cutting school, smoking, and hanging with the wrong crowd! I need your help, and I need it NOW!" I actually could not believe my ears.

My first thought was to tell her, "You made this bed, now lie in it!" Yet I listened and then prayed for wisdom. What was the wise thing to do? The answer was clear. If I did not act now, this child could end up in jail, or worse. I realized this was not the time to beat the drum that I was right, but rather this was the time when we needed to work together to parent her and not let her pit us against each other.

As I prayed for wisdom, the first answer I got was to establish ground rules stating that this could not happen again. I told her mother that I would only consider helping if she was willing to give me full, legal custody. She quickly said yes. Then I told her I would have to talk with Dee and get back to her.

To say that was a difficult conversation is a huge understatement. Dee made it clear that she was not happy about bringing Sherry back. She said that our house was calm and drama free, and she didn't want to go back to the spectacle of what we had experienced before. Dee also said that Sherry often reminded her that she was not her mom and that her mother told her she did not have to do what Dee said. Dee feared that the anger Sherry expressed toward her would play out in her being less than loving to her little brother, William. Dee said that we should let her mother grow up and handle this situation, since she created it.

We talked it over, back and forth, and I listened to her perspective. As I said, nine times out of ten, I went with Dee's perspective because she was my trusted advisor. This time was different, however. As I had prayed for wisdom, I kept getting the same answer: I needed to go get this girl and save her from herself. Plus, I kept hearing that as the head of the household I needed to make the call even if it was uncomfortable. I told Dee that I had decided that we needed to go get Sherry. Dee said okay, but I knew she was concerned about what would happen when Sherry came back.

Now I really needed wisdom. The Bible states that wisdom is the primary thing to search for. "The one who gets wisdom loves life; the one who cherishes understanding will soon prosper" (Proverbs 19:8; NIV). So, I prayed and decided to seek wisdom. I called my mother and sought her wisdom, and she recommended I continue to talk to my wife and also keep praying, because God would make a way.

Then God intervened. Dee called her mother and shared what was going on. Dee's mother was a Godly woman and one of the wisest people I have ever met. She counseled Dee and asked her two simple questions. First, "Dee, would you want to be married to a man who would not take care of his children?" And second, "If anything, happened to you, and Willie had a similar situation with William, would you want him to desert him just because it was uncomfortable?" Those questions helped Dee change her perspective. She then told me I was right and agreed that we had to go get Sherry. God gave me confirmation, through Dee's mom, that I had made the right decision.

We went to get Sherry, signed the custody papers, and brought her back to D.C. The next few months were extremely challenging. Sherry would not talk to us. She would come down for meals, then march back upstairs, and slam the door. Aside from eating meals and going to school, she did not leave her room. I would occasionally remind her that I now had custody, and I would also remind myself to be patient. Her mother was no longer able to come and steal her away. I just prayed and waited for her to let go of her anger. In time, my prayers were answered, and she became pleasant. I believe one of the keys to her change in attitude came from the daily ride to school. During those thirty minutes to and from school, Dee played motivational tapes in the car. Eventually their messages began to sink in. Another key to Sherry's improved attitude came from our church policy: everyone who eats and sleeps in our house must go with us to church on Sunday.

In time, church did its work.

In all these years of marriage, bringing Sherry home to live with us again was one of the few times I had to use my veto power. I felt it was necessary to use my veto power, but I was very slow to use it and made a point to pray and seek God first.

Just as I promised never to abuse that veto power, there was another important part to the success of our decision-making process. Once the decision was made, Dee was all in. Again, we work together as a team to make each decision a success. She is always by my side, helping me work things out. And when the circumstances don't turn out the way I think they should, Dee never says, "I told you so." She always has my back.

Dee has earned my trust, and I have earned hers. Because we always talk everything through before I use that veto power, I know her concerns and fears, and she knows mine. The fact that she's been able to actively support me in those decisions, even after having voiced all her concerns, was a game changer in our relationship. She is, hands down, my most trusted advisor.

I interviewed a friend at church who has been happily married for more than forty years, and he shared a humorous perspective about how he handled tough decisions in his marriage. He said that when they got married, he informed his wife that he was the head of the household and he would therefore make all the major decisions, and she would handle all the minor decisions. He said, "It's amazing, but in forty years there have been no major decisions!" In other words, she made all the decisions! Then he remarked, he was the ultimate head of the household and always had the last word. Always! He asked me if I wanted to know what he would say, and I said yes. He said the last word was usually the same each time: "Yes, dear!"

DEE'S PERSPECTIVE

Willie and I had many conversations about why we should not get married. Well, actually, he listened as I came up with the excuses:

- You've never lived on your own.
- You live with your mother.
- You sing for your supper.
- You've never been responsible for household finances.

I thought Willie needed more experience in living alone before getting married. I had been married before and realized marriage could be challenging, especially in the areas of communicating, compromising, and being considerate of each other.

Then, there was the head of the household issue. Was I willing to let Willie be the head of the household? I knew that men had the biblical responsibility to be the head of the household—I was a preacher's kid! But I was not feeling that.

It meant I was not going to make all the decisions I had gotten used to making. It also meant being respectful of his views and—worst of all—compromising. Willie even thought it meant sharing my daily schedule with him. What?! Why did Willie need to know when I was leaving work, heading to the gym, shoe shopping, or perusing the veggie section of my favorite health food store? I had been single and calling my own shots for so long that I was stuck in doing everything my own way.

Head and Neck

When Willie said, "You are already a successful business-woman. You manage your own household. Certainly, you can run ours. Just let me think I'm in charge." That's when I realized I could consider this marriage arrangement. Of course, I then asked, "Now, what does that look like to you?" We discussed it, and his main concern was respect. Respect is critical for men. I did respect him, so I said, "I can make you feel like you're in charge, just like mom did with my dad." My dad was the head of the household, but my Mom ran everything. As my mom would say, "Your father is the head of the household, but I am the neck. And the head cannot turn without the neck." So Willie and I adopted this mindset as a working team, and it has worked well for over thirty years.

MY ATTITUDE, MY CHOICE

Frankly, the use of Willie's veto power proved to be more of a challenge than I had anticipated. I had always been able to use logic and wisely placed emotional arguments to get Willie to see my perspective on most issues. Sherry's return to our home was emotionally disastrous for me. I remembered how painful it was to live with a person who refused to acknowledge I even existed. When she returned, I wondered if she would be mean to her little brother, William as well.

Although my mom had helped me to see that Willie's decision was the only right course of action, I had to work on my attitude to honestly be "all in" with Willie on the decision. It's easy to care for someone when they are pleasant to you, but with Sherry back in our home, I had to pray for a lot of grace: grace to be pleasant, grace to hold my tongue and say nothing when I wanted to scream, and grace to understand Sherry and what she was "growing" through. I prayed for wisdom on how to support my husband as he struggled to develop his parenting wisdom. (Often, just being by his side was all I could do.) I prayed to become a Proverbs 31 woman. I needed the heart of a loving wife and mother who could love without conditions and adjust graciously as the circumstances demanded.

Honoring Willie's veto power forced me to mature emotionally. It did not matter how I felt. What did matter was following the right course of action for our family. Once that decision was made, I had to help make that decision successful, which meant disciplining myself emotionally to make that happen. Yes, I definitely matured during those years. I earned the right to be called Willie's trusted advisor!

Do You Need to Be Right or Do You Want to Be Happy?

I believe another reason Willie and I have a strong and happy marriage is that we have considered whether we need to be right all the time or happy. Think about it. Do you need to win the argument or are you willing to create a win-win mindset for both of you? Wise couples agree that peace and happiness is much more important than getting one's way all the time. The more you create harmony in your marriage, the more you can focus on the goals and dreams you want to achieve together. In pursuing this mindset, we adopted the sayings: "Happy wife, happy life. Happy man, that's the plan. Happy spouse, happy house." Though these are cute phrases, we actually believe them. And as we love and trust each other, we have learned that we do not need to be right all the time. The more we succeed as a unit, the more we realize we are in this together.

♥ JOLLEY ADVICE

1. **Agree in advance to listen to each other's perspective.** In time, you will develop your household's own trusted-advisor system.
2. **Agree that veto power will never be abused, and only used rarely.**
3. **Once a decision is made, everyone in the household must be all in for the decision to succeed.**
4. **Never say the words "I told you so."**

♥

CHAPTER EIGHT

Sex, Headaches, and Other Lies

"Love (and Marriage) is an ice-cream sundae,
with all the marvelous coverings,
and sex is the cherry on the top."
~ Jimmy Dean

WILLIE'S PERSPECTIVE

This book is entitled, *Make Love, Make Money, Make It Last!* So far, we have primarily talked about how to make it last. But one of the most important parts of making a marriage last is making love, and making love often involves sex. So let's talk about SEX!

Sex is a powerful and important part of marriage, but if it gets out of balance, it can destroy your marriage. One way couples get out of balance is when they think sex is all you need to have a great marriage. That is simply not true. No matter how great the sex, there has to be more to keep a marriage healthy. No one stays in bed twenty-four hours a day. Life demands family time, working, eating, sleeping, and exercising. Marriage is a multidimensional experience. It is friendship, love and respect, companionship, intellectual stimulation, laughter, and much more.

Years ago, a couple who was having marital problems invited us to dinner at an exclusive restaurant in D.C. to discuss their situation. Almost as soon as they sat down, they started arguing. They said they argued all the time, they blamed each other for their problems. They argued about who should pay the mortgage note. They argued about the division of labor in the household. They argued about his decision to become an entrepreneur and the fluctuating income that came along with that. They argued about her corporate job and how she had to work long hours. They argued about almost everything—that is, until they talked about sex. When they brought up their sex life, everything changed and they became lovey-dovey.

From the moment they focused on their sex life, they looked longingly at each other and talked about how much they enjoyed each other's touch. The more they talked about their sex life, the nicer they were to each other. It didn't take us long to realize they had gotten married for one reason and one reason only: sex! Aside from sex, there was nothing substantive about their union. They certainly were not best friends. They were not even in love with each other as people, but rather as sex partners. They loved the sexual satisfaction they received from each other, but nothing else. Sex is awesome, but it is not enough to maintain a happy marriage.

We advised them to get professional marriage counseling, but they did not. They continued with their sex-based marriage, and continued to argue about everything, except sex. Eventually they got divorced because there was nothing other than sex holding the core of their relationship together. There was no mutual respect, no shared values, no shared dreams, no willingness to sit and reason together, and no enjoying time together in each other's presence, outside of the bedroom.

While Dee and I enjoy the sexual aspects of our marriage, it is a result of really enjoying each other outside of the bedroom. We respect and appreciate the differences we each bring to our relationship. We complement each other. I am the macro, the big picture guy, while Dee is the micro, she focuses on the details. Or as we like to say, I am the tree shaker, she is the jelly maker. We work together and are each other's best friend. While sex is important, it is just a valued piece of our greater relationship.

Longtime friends of ours, Tim and Rhonda Smith, shared with us that over the years they were always curious when friends informed them that they were getting divorced; so they asked them questions to find out why. Tim and Rhonda often asked how their sex lives were during their marriages. In each instance, the couples said that they had stopped having sex within the year before they divorced.

While it's certainly an unscientific poll, it might suggest that the sexual aspect of their relationship disappeared well before the marriage ended. We, therefore, believe that the lack of intimacy (being pleasant, talking sweetly to each other, cuddling, holding hands, and valuing each other's opinion) probably played a major role in the demise of their sex lives, and then their overall married lives.

Intimacy vs. Sex

Sex and intimacy are often thought to be the same thing, but they are not. Sex is a physical act, intimacy is emotional. Most often, intimacy occurs outside of the bedroom. For Dee, that means being physically and emotionally close to her. Things such as holding hands, sitting close, touching, talking, calling to tell her I miss her, and just spending time in her presence are all important to her sense of intimacy. Even as busy professionals, you can take a moment to leave a loving voicemail or send a simple loving text message or emoji to your spouse. This does not mean always having sexual intercourse. You can have intimacy when you have sex, but you don't have to have sex to have intimacy.

I've learned that if I pay attention to Dee's need for intimacy during the day, it has a positive impact on what happens at night. If our level of intimacy meets her needs, she feels secure and sex is a very natural by-product. Therefore, I've learned that romance starts from the neck up. That said, men, I recommend you take heed to this piece of information: if you want more sex, you should work on the intimacy factor.

A comedian shared a joke about love. On a young man's wedding day, he told his new bride he loved her, but he never repeated those words again! When asked many years later, why he never again said, "I love you," he responded, "I told her on our wedding day and figured if I ever changed my mind, I'd let her know!" That joke got a big laugh from the audience. But I can assure you, if he hadn't told his wife he loved her since his wedding day, he's missed out on a lot of sex.

Security

Besides intimacy, I have learned that women also need security. By security, I mean safety and protection. Women need to know that you can and will take care of them, financially, spiritually, and intimately. Before we married, Dee was an independent woman, slaying her own dragons (she had a career, a fancy sports car, and an uptown apartment), but my presence in her life enriched all of that. I appreciate her and respect her professional life. To this day, I make a point of making her laugh, telling her she is beautiful inside and out and reminding her of how sexy she is to me.

I use my words to actively weave myself into her life until she wants me around all the time.

Be A Promise Keeper

One way we create security is by keeping promises. Do you remember that I promised Dee if she would live in my mother's attic for one year, I would buy her a house in Washington, D.C.? I explained that living rent-free would allow us to save quickly and grow a bigger deposit for the home we wanted to buy. I kept my word and worked hard to make her secure. The more I do what I say I will do and show Dee I love her, the sweeter my life becomes. I have kept my promises and it has meant the world to Dee, providing the security that is so important to her.

Intimacy and security are two of the most powerful forces to make your wife happy. Dee and I work together, travel together, and spend leisure time together. When I walk across the hall to her office, I may kiss her on the cheek, touch her hand, or give her a squeeze. I enjoy any time with her. And I love the rewards I get for all that attention I give her! Gents, I am telling you, if you want more romance, you need to create more intimate moments with your wife, while making her feel secure.

WHAT MEN NEED: SEX AND RESPECT!

Just as most women need two critical things—intimacy and security—most men need two things—sex and respect Where women need intimacy, which is emotionally based, men need sex, which is physically based. For men, sex is a basic physical need, like food and sleep!

A study was done for The Journal of Sex Research and reprinted in Psychology Today by lead author Dr. Terri D.

Fisher, a professor of psychology at Ohio State University. The study asked men to rank the ideas they thought about most often, and sex was number one.

According to the study, men thought about sex approximately nineteen times per day. That is how men are wired.

As one of my friends said to me, "You know the old saying, 'happy wife, happy life.' Well there is also one for men: 'for a happy man, sex is the plan.'" For more proof that sex is important to men, I was at a men's gathering, and the issue of sex was a major topic of conversation throughout the day. One gentleman put it this way: "Sex is not the answer. Sex is the question, and YES is the answer!" Everyone laughed, but everyone in the room agreed. Sex is a major issue for men!

Most women do not think about sex anywhere nearly as often as men do. Some women even dismiss the importance of sex in marriage. They may feel that since they're married, it's no longer a big deal, or they're no longer excited about having sex with their husbands. They may have been the boss at work all day, prepared dinner, helped the children with homework, and now just cuddling or sleeping is all they want. They may even pretend to be asleep! Or they may use that age-old lie, "I have a headache."

Having a headache is not a good choice. My friend, professional speaker and bestselling author Jane Herlong, shared the advice her mom gave her on the eve of her wedding to her husband Thomas: "Now that you're getting married, don't ever tell that lie that you've got a headache. 'Cause there's a woman somewhere who has an aspirin in her pocketbook!"

SEX IS NOT A WEAPON

Sex can be a terrific reward, but it should never be used as a weapon. Never withhold sex to retaliate or hurt your spouse.

It will always backfire. Withholding sex is a mistake because it leads people to seek other ways to satisfy their sexual needs. Often those options are not good for the person's long-term happiness, and they're definitely not good for the relationship or the marriage.

Sex is a beautiful and wonderful part of marriage, and while it can be an effective tool for influencing your spouse, it should never be used as a weapon. I am not the neatest one in the household. When my gym bag, towels, pants, several pairs of shoes and underwear, and my tennis racket expand to the middle of our bedroom floor, Dee does not fuss. She knows I am messy. Even when we travel, I request a room with double beds; then I unpack and throw everything all over the second bed. I'm very happy being messy! But when Dee's had enough and needs some organization, she simply says, "Honey, just hide all that stuff in the closet, please; I won't look in there. And I'll reward you for your job well done!" I know exactly what that means, so I quickly clean up the mess.

Dee influences me, and makes me want to straighten up, even though it's not in my nature. She positively reinforces me. We both know the drill and we both like the outcome—intimacy and sex. Sex is a terrific motivator for the motivator—me!

Also, it is important to note that men do not always have to be the ones to initiate sex. Ladies, you can be the initiator as well. It is great for a woman to be the romantic aggressor. And men, if you are still operating with that old paradigm that men must always initiate sex, you should evaluate your self-esteem. Be excited that your spouse wants to chase you. Dee chases me, and I love it!

TEMPTATION

Faithfulness is a decision. One of the most important parts of marriage is making wise decisions. Marriages can be destroyed when a spouse decides to be unfaithful. With temptations all around, how do you handle it?

My friend Kevin Toney, a Grammy nominated jazz piano player and founding member of the hit group the Blackbyrds, wrote a book entitled Breaking the Men's Code. He grew up in Detroit, in a time when it was fashionable for men to have a "chick on the side." When Kevin got married, he continued with the men's code he had been taught by his father and uncles, and it almost ruined his marriage and, even worse, his life. Thankfully, he had a friend who refused to lie for him when Kevin used the friend as an alibi. Kevin was forced to confess to his wife that he had been unfaithful. He was very thankful that his wife was willing to go with him to counseling; they had a spiritual renewal that changed their lives and sustained their marriage. They agreed that their faith in Jesus Christ was the key to renewing their marriage.

For years, I traveled by myself, while Dee was at home raising our children. There were many opportunities to stray, but I used a business strategy I learned that works great under any circumstance. It's called the Wise Decision-Making Formula.

There are four questions I recommend you ask yourself if you have temptations that make you think about stepping outside your marriage.

Question #1: What is the best that can happen if I make the decision to step outside my marriage?

Question #2: What is the worst that can happen if I make this decision?

Question #3: What is the most likely thing to happen if I make this decision?

Question #4: Am I willing to live with the worst to get to the best?

Let's use me as an example. If I'm on the road and a woman makes advances toward me, what would my process look like?

Question #1: What would be the best that would happen?
A night of sex!

Question #2: What is the worst that can happen?
I could lose my wife!

Question #3: What is the most likely thing to happen?
A one-night stand, a short-lived affair, yet a lingering question in my mind that this might come back to haunt me, including the fear that my wife would somehow find out.

Question #4: Am I willing to live with the worst to get to the best? Am I willing to lose my wife, the woman I worked so hard to woo and marry, who is also my best friend, for a quick roll in the hay with someone I really don't love and who might end up becoming my worst nightmare? (Think about the movie Fatal Attraction.)

And when I went through that decision-making process, the answer was always simple: absolutely not!

When we got married Dee said that she expected me to be faithful, because she knew my character. That said, she believed that sometimes men lose their minds, so she made it clear to me that unfaithfulness would not work for her. She never threatened to kill me if I was unfaithful; she said she would not look good in stripes. Rather, she mentioned super glue, and body parts. She said if I could not keep my key parts for cleaving with her, then she would be forced to cleave them permanently to me.

All jokes aside, I have seen marriages destroyed over sex, whether that's due to not enough sex, a lack of intimacy, or sex outside of the marriage. I have seen those issues for both men and women; all of these issues can cut both ways. Understand that sex is powerful and wonderful, and it can be an incredible aspect of the marriage experience. Like anything else that is powerful (i.e., a nuclear weapon or super-charged sports car), it needs to be handled with care and wisdom.

DEE'S PERSPECTIVE

I can't think of a time since we've been married that I didn't want to be around Willie. That sounds funny now as I reflect on the beginning of our relationship, when I told Willie we could be nothing more than friends.

DEVELOP THE FRIENDSHIP BEFORE INTIMACY

Willie was thoughtful, friendly, funny, and easy to be around. He was patient and wise in how he handled my "not interested" attitude. Over time, he slowly became my best friend. Up to that point, my very best friends had always been my parents. I talked to them daily about one thing or another. They were my champions and made me believe that I was capable of changing the world. Then came this new person —Willie—who slowly moved my parents out of first place and became my confidante.

Willie helped me to not take myself so seriously and encouraged me to find the humor in life, and have fun. Who knew he could get me to take a vacation and even a day cruise on a catamaran, when I don't swim and don't particularly like boats! Willie had gained my trust and made me feel safe, and I had fallen in love with him. We shared the same values and viewed the world the same way, such as our love for our parents, love of God, love of learning, and love of just being in each other's presence. Willie always made me feel secure, loved, comfortable, and special. This made it very easy to communicate with him on all different levels, and I view intimacy and sex as communication at the highest levels.

Willie had always been in business for himself—first the music business, then the speaking business. He is a true entrepreneur and loves it. I understood the entrepreneurial world because my parents had successfully operated their own businesses. This made it easy for me to adjust to Willie's hectic work schedule; he was always working on one thing or another—just like my parents!

Enter Their World

But the thought of us being entrepreneurs together was frightening, and I wanted no part of it. I was happy and comfortable with my good government job on Capitol Hill. Willie never forced me into the "family" business of speaking and training, but he surely did influence me to come into his world. He would read a business book, share his excitement about it, and then say, "I want your opinion" or "I would love to get your take on it." Once I read the books he shared, I started to get a better understanding of how and why he thought the way he did and why he was so gung-ho on being an entrepreneur. Later, Willie asked if I would listen to motivational audios and give him my feedback. Again, after listening I was motivated and inspired. He would ask me to proofread his articles and books, and again I would be uplifted. Slowly, he drew me into his motivational and personal development world.

Finally, he talked me into coming to work with him part-time. I started working with him one day a week, then two days, then three days, until I worked with Willie four days a week and my Capitol Hill job only one day a week. I slowly became a full-time entrepreneur. He got me to take a leap of faith and be brave. There was still a fear of the leap, but I did it. Willie convinced me that we could be more successful building the business together. He had influenced me and positively changed my perspective on business. He got me to buy into his vision of the world and do what he often says in his speeches: "to jump... and grow wings on the way!"

Create Special Moments

How—exactly—did he manage to do that? He created special moments for us that were more than physical; they were intimate, loving, and secure. One example is how he made me feel that my opinions were of great value. He continually asked for my input and business ideas. This made me feel secure in my importance in his business and personal life, and all the while, he was educating and teaching me how to become an entrepreneur. This made it very enjoyable to communicate with him on many different levels—in business as well as personally with intimacy, friendship and sex.

I now realize Willie was persuading me to join the high-wire act of entrepreneurism. And I chose to do so willingly even though I was afraid because he had kindled in me that unconditional love and desire to support him and be a part of every aspect of his life. Although we might stumble or occasionally lose our grip on the high wire, we keep traversing it together. We carry each other, encourage each other, and love each other, no matter the circumstances. It is not based on the conditions, but is based on love.

Unconditional Love

There is a song entitled, "A Thousand Years," by Christine Perri. The lyrics express that you feel so connected to a person, you believe you've loved them forever - a thousand years. And yet they inspire you still, so you want to give them more love - for a thousand more! You've been through challenges together. You've laughed together. You've trusted together. You know each other. And yet, you still chose to love and respect each other with all that history you have! That's unconditional love. Just as Jesus loves, that is how the song says, we should love.

COMMUNICATING YOUR FEELINGS, NEEDS, FRUSTRATIONS

When Willie and I first began seeing each other, I was not comfortable sharing my feelings openly. I have always been introspective and reserved, but Willie helped me to learn that true friends share their feelings with each other. They are vulnerable with each other, and they commiserate together by sharing special moments that others just don't get. They work hard on understanding each other.

With that in mind, I made a conscious decision to work on communicating my thoughts, fears, frustrations, and exactly what I was thinking and feeling. This was very hard for me to do because I had always been an introvert. I learned to share my feelings with Willie because he took the time to listen to my thoughts and ideas, which is huge for me. I would practice what I wanted to say to Willie in my head first (often, for hours), until I felt I could express exactly what I was feeling, and he listened. Sharing my innermost thoughts is easy now because I have practiced it over the years with him.

Tips for Effective Communication with your Wife

Here are tips for men as they communicate with women:

1. Just take time to listen.
2. Don't jump to conclusions.
3. Don't try to fix the problem.
4. Don't even search for solutions.
5. Just listen, acknowledge, and sit quietly, absorbing the words. This style of listening means a lot to women.

If you're not accustomed to or comfortable in sharing your feelings during the most intimate moments, then practice. There are some phrases you can use to help yourself: "I need to talk about this, but it is uncomfortable, so please be patient with me" or "This is what I am thinking" or "This is how you made me feel earlier, and this is how it makes me feel now."

Additionally, if you don't know your spouse's love language, you must find out. Both of you should read Gary Chapman's book *The Five Love Languages: How to Express Heartfelt Commitment to Your Mate*. It will give you the tools you need to discover each other's love language: is it words of affirmation, acts of service, gifts, quality time, or physical touch? The right combination of each other's love languages will produce wonderful intimacy, which leads to great sex. In essence, find out what pleases your spouse and tell them what pleases you. Then get busy!

Again, intimacy and sex are not the same. For instance, I like it when Willie and I sit together and talk. He listens to me and affirms my feelings and thoughts. When Willie listens to me intently, it makes me feel wanted and it increases my romantic feelings. Men, please listen to your wives. And ladies, I encourage you to think carefully about the words you speak before you share them with your husband. Be clear, kind, respectful, accurate and loving in your communication. This will help you and your spouse keep the loving feeling going and growing.

SEXLESS?

While an active sex life is usually seen as an important part of a healthy marriage, according to The Aspen Institute for the Study of Family and Culture, 20 percent of married people had not had sex during the last month; 12 percent hadn't had sex in three months, and 6 percent had not had sex in over a year. This data is from the Institute's "Relationships in America" survey, which sampled married adults ages 18-60. And according to data scientist Seth Stephens-Davidowitz, "sexless marriage" is one of **the most frequently searched phrases on the internet.**

Why do I bring this up? Because a vibrant sex life varies depending on the circumstances of the couple. New York City sex therapist Ian Kerner says that our sexuality evolves in response to our age, health, hormones, and lifestyle changes. This means it is imperative for the two of you to talk, agree on, and continuously work on your own special rhythm for intimacy and sex. Once a month may work for your relationship.

If you have mismatched libidos, it is wisest for you to seek professional counseling with the goal of working out a solution.

THE "THREE-S MARRIAGE SUCCESS SYSTEM"

Jerry Jasinowski is Willie's long-time tennis partner. Jerry and his wife, Isabel, have been married for over forty years, and they have a simple, yet powerful viewpoint on marriage, which they call the three S's. Jerry shared the advice he gave to a gentleman sitting next to him on a flight. The man had been married and divorced four times and expressed that he did not believe it was possible to have a happy, healthy, and successful marriage. Jerry explained that the man's thinking was part of the reason that his marriages didn't work. His marriages did not succeed because he had negative expectations, meaning that each failed marriage was a self-fulfilling prophecy. Jerry said, "If you are not expecting it to last, then you're preparing for it to fail." And most often you will get exactly what you expect.

Sweet

Jerry told the gentleman to remember these three S's for a successful marriage: sweet, smart, and sexy. "Start with your heart" said Jerry, pointing to his heart. That denotes "be sweet!" Great relationships and marriages start with someone who is your friend and who is nice to you, and vice versa. You want a relationship with someone you can trust your heart to and who values that trust. Be sweet to each other. Be kind to each other. Be nice to each other. Start with the heart.

Smart

For the second S, Jerry pointed to his head. "Be smart," he said. You must be smart in choosing your mate. Love alone is not enough to maintain a long-term marriage. Love is important, but you need an intelligent person that you enjoy being with and that you can engage in meaningful conversation with. The person you choose to marry needs to intellectually stimulate you as well as emotionally and physically stimulate you.

Sexy

That leads to the third S, and with this point Jerry pointed to his pelvic region. "The last S stands for be sexy!" The person you marry should turn you on sexually. Jerry says, "Marriage based purely on sex is probably not going to last, but a marriage without sex is probably not going to last either." If it does, it won't have the fullness and intimacy it could, or should, have. Sex is important and the marriages that last, while being completely fulfilling are those that understand the importance of sex and how it is not just a physical act, but an act of love and commitment. Remember the Three S's: "Be Sweet, Be Smart and Be Sexy!"

♥ JOLLEY ADVICE
1. **Never have a headache.**
2. **Never use sex as a weapon to get back at your spouse.**
3. **If you are having a sexual or performance problem, get professional help.**
4. **Women, be open to help stimulate your husband.**
5. **Men, talk to your mate about what she likes.** Remember, it's not all about you.
6. **Remember that intimacy is important for women.** "If you want sex at night, start working on it that morning."
7. **Memorize the decision-making formula to keep you from yielding to temptation.**

MAKE LOVE, MAKE MONEY, MAKE IT LAST!

♥

CHAPTER NINE

Always Date Your Mate

"A husband should never stop dating his wife,
and a wife should never stop flirting with her husband!
~ Aysha Ghaly

WILLIE'S PERSPECTIVE

If you want to keep the fires burning in your relationship after the honeymoon, you must continue to date your spouse. Do this and you'll keep the marriage fresh and fun while you strengthen the bonds of your friendship, love, and trust.

Early in our marriage, an older couple advised us to do two things: continue to hold hands and have a date night every week. They said, "One day your children will grow up and leave home. If you don't sustain your relationship during those child-raising years, you'll find yourselves as two strangers in the same house."

Lo and behold, the older couple was right! Our children did grow up, go to college, and then go on to careers in different cities. When they left the nest, we did not have to re-introduce ourselves to each other because we had maintained our relationship during the child-raising years. Today, we still hold hands and still have a weekly date night, even though we are together every day.

Every day is a date for us, but we still have a specific time set aside for our date night every Thursday night. We might even do something as simple as going to Walmart on our date night. It does not matter what the activity is as long as we are intentionally together and focused on our relationship. Whether we watch TV or just go for a walk and hold hands, it is still our date night. The result is that after more than thirty years, we still have a lot to talk about and we still enjoy being around each other. But we don't take that for granted. We know date night helped us build that loving relationship.

We often ask couples we counsel these questions: When you were first dating, were you excited about each other? Did you enjoy spending time together? Did you hold hands or walk arm in arm? If the answer is yes, then do you still do the same things today? If not, why not? What has changed?

Why Relationships Change

What typically changes in a marriage is that the couple forgot what brought them to the altar. Usually, it was because of all the other things that happened along the way: kids, bills, sickness, careers, and so forth. As a result, they stopped dating. The family responsibilities and stresses are exactly why it's important to continue to date. With children, your life becomes more hectic and the children can become the whole focus of your time and energy. This can cause you to lose your intimate relationship. To help prevent this, we highly recommend a weekly date night. This weekly date time offers precious moments for the two of you to focus on each other rather than the kids.

Manage a Weekly Date Night

When we first started having a weekly date night, there was no money in the budget for an evening out. So, we improvised, and our date night was held in our bedroom. We would sit on the bench in our room and watch our favorite shows, Hill Street Blues, LA Law, and then ER. The door to our bedroom stayed open during our Thursday night date, but the kids could not come in, unless there was an emergency. We sat with a bag of popcorn, talked, and watched our shows. The only off-limits topic was the kids, since we talked about them almost every hour of the day. Instead of talking about them, we talked about us, and what was happening in our individual lives. Even when I started speaking and traveling, we maintained our Thursday night ritual. I would call Dee from my hotel room and we would talk and watch TV, just as if we were at home together.

Additionally, it is important to have date nights even when you do not have children. Couples can often have hectic business and social lives. It becomes easy for couples to lose track of why they are together in the first place. Date nights counteract that and allow for there to be time spent and intimacy built to remind you of your love for each other.

Power of Holding Hands

The older couple was also right in regards to holding hands. They said, "When you hold hands, you're not just touching hands, but really touching each other's hearts." Holding hands has had a tremendous impact on our relationship. When we travel people often comment that we must be newlyweds because we hold hands as we walk through airports. I often respond, "Yes, we're newlyweds…thirty plus years and we're just getting started." This must be love because when I was single, I would never hold hands with the lady I was out with—never! That was too much of a commitment, and could give the wrong impression. Yet, when I got married, I was very happy to show the world that I was serious and committed to Dee, and we've never stopped holding hands.

Some years ago, we were out for a walk around our neighborhood, talking and holding hands. A man we did not know rode past us, stopped, backed up, rolled down his window, clapped, and said, "Wow! I love that! I am going to start doing that too." We can influence others not only with our words, but when we walk our talk.

SAY IT!

Tell your spouse you love them, every day. When you say, "I love you," you strengthen your connections and keep the fires burning. Some days you will not feel like saying it, but say it anyway. It is like medicine for your spirit, mind, and heart. Treat it like bathing - do it daily.

Your words have power, for either good or bad, so speak good into your life and marriage. Husbands, talk about how you love your wife, and wives, talk about how you love your husband. Speak it even when you are not quite feeling it, and keep speaking it. Scripture says that faith comes by hearing. The more you hear something, the more your faith in that item grows. The same is true for love; it also grows by hearing, specifically, from hearing the words "I love you." The more you hear it, the more you feel it. Once I figured this out, I made a point to tell Dee every day.

Men, women need to hear you say, "I love you." The more you say it, the better your wife will feel, and the more you hear it coming from your own lips, the more your love for her will be reinforced. Faith comes by hearing, even if you are the one saying it. The more you hear it, the more you will believe it, and the more you believe it, the more you will act like it. So keep saying "I love you," because it works.

WHO LOVES WHO MORE?

The concept of who loves who more is built around the idea of a seesaw. In any relationship, the person who loves the least is the person in power. At that moment, the person who loves the least has an advantage over the person who has a longing for the other. Yet, the best relationships are the ones in which the power is always shifting back and forth, just like children on a seesaw. In our marriage, the power is always shifting. Today, I love Dee more. Tomorrow she loves me more. It's just like a seesaw going up and down!

One of our marriage secrets is that Dee and I are in a competition as to who can love the other more. In order to do this, we work on how we show our love to each other on a daily basis. This can be expressed in very simple ways. For instance, I bring Dee a cup of coffee in the afternoon when I know she is focused on a project and probably won't stop to get a cup for herself. In turn, Dee often surprises me with a homemade smoothie, which she knows I love.

I wrote about this concept of who loves who more in my first book, *It Only Takes A Minute To Change Your Life!*, there's a chapter that says, "What's love got to do with it? EVERYTHING!" Here are a few excerpts from that chapter.

SAY "I LOVE YOU"...EVERYDAY!

We talked earlier about how to communicate more effectively with our spouse. Now let me share another secret that I have found to be most helpful. I make it a part of my daily routine to tell my wife I love her. And it's that simple. That is one of the secrets to our success. I have found there are days when I love her more than she loves me, and days when she loves me more than I love her. Because of this, we have a relationship where the power is constantly shifting. We have found that the person who loves the least in any relationship has more power than the one who loves the most. Therefore, the best relationships are the ones where the power is constantly shifting and vacillating from one person to another. Every day, whether I love her more or whether she loves me more, I make it a point to tell her I love her. Not only does it make her feel more secure, but it also reminds me of my decision to be in love. Remember: love is not just an emotion; it is a decision!

THE MAGIC FORMULA OF WINNING RELATIONSHIPS

Almost every day I am asked what is the secret to having a successful and enjoyable relationship. My wife and I not only live together, but also work and play together. Many people marvel at how much we enjoy each other's presence. What is our secret? The secret is we work on loving each other daily.

I remember talking to a couple who had been married more than fifty years who gave me advice as I was preparing for my wedding day. They told me to remember that "love is more than an emotion; it is a decision. When you say I do, then do" Second, we talk about everything, not some things... but everything! When we have a problem, we talk about it immediately. And we work it out so that no one loses. We go for win-wins, so we both win. We learned that we do not have to argue. Instead, we can talk about it. We talk "to" each other and not "at" each other. And since we talk to each other, we are much less likely to argue, as it takes two people to argue.

Remember, you both have a choice. You can talk to each other, which is communication, or at each other, which leads to confrontation. If confrontation is not diffused by consideration, then that can lead to arguments, fussing, and fighting, which is an altercation. In altercations, many people want to win so badly that they won't let it die. Each side wants the last word, which leads to constant retaliation. Then things are said in a moment of heated conversation that makes it impossible for reconciliation, which leads to a breakup and non-communication.

Why go through all of that drama? Have a little patience and talk to each other. Learn to talk to each other and not at each other. Life will be much sweeter!

Here is a take on marriage that focuses on taking time and care of your marriage. It is the belief that marriage is like grass. If watered, your grass stays green. If neglected, your grass withers and eventually dies. Everyone loves a beautiful lawn, but most people are unwilling to do the work it takes to keep the grass beautiful. An old saying states that the grass is always greener on the other side—most likely because the grass on the other side is watered and fertilized. Yet, most people who I talk to who have great lawns don't talk about the work it takes, but the love it takes. And the longer they do the work, the easier the maintenance gets! The same is true for marriage. To have a great marriage takes effort. And sometimes the word work is used, but those who do it successfully don't see it as work, but rather as a labor of love. And the longer you do the work, that labor of love, the easier it gets and the sweeter it is.

DEE'S PERSPECTIVE

The purchase of our home came one year after we had moved into my mother-in-law's attic—rent-free of course! Our "new" home was built in 1912 with a large wraparound porch, including nine colonial style columns, very distinctive stucco exterior finishing, and lots of big drafty single-pane windows.

The very first winter we spent in our house, blasts of cold wind whipped around the porch's columns, slapped that stucco siding, and seeped into the house's single-pane windows. In response, Willie and I turned up the heat without a care in the world. We loved our new home and enjoyed the warmth. We walked around the house in short sleeves. That is, until the first heating bill arrived, which was over seven hundred dollars! Sweaters became our attire around the house, and Home Depot became our new best friend. We bought large sheets of plastic to stretch over the windows, using tape and hair dryers to attach and tighten the plastic.

We were both working outside of the home and decided to hire a nanny. We reasoned at the time that a nanny was less expensive than daycare and she could perform light house-keeping chores and prepare dinners. She did not last. Not only was she not attentive to household details, but she had a bad attitude when we told her about the things she'd overlooked. Our baby boy, William, had a diaper rash. His room was never tidy. The diaper pail overflowed. And there was always an excuse why dinner was not ready. On top of that, she was costing me half my monthly take-home pay!

Moreover, Willie's schedule did not mesh with mine. At the time, he was singing in nightclubs until two in the morning, and then working in his recording studio during the day. I was up and out well before he rose. This was not the environment for creating the loving, thriving Christian home that I had envisioned when I said, "I do," to my nightclub-singing, jingle-recording husband. There was never time to talk, and we had plenty of things to talk about! We needed to figure out how to budget for the unplanned heating bills, decide on the right childcare for our son, coordinate after-school care for our middle school daughter, and make time for our family and our faith.

During this time, an older couple recommended we have a date night, and it sounded like a good solution to our problem. I thought, "Whoo-Whee...time alone!" After we worked on our jobs, worked with the kids, and worked on the house, we needed time alone to work on our relationship. Best of all, it did not cost a penny, which was a good thing because we didn't have any extra pennies to spend on going out for a date.

Every Thursday night you could find us in our bedroom with the door open, sitting on the little sofa at the foot of our bed. The children could walk by, but not come in. Mom and Dad were having time alone together to work on our friendship and our marriage relationship.

On those date nights we talked about our relationship and enjoyed just being in each other's presence. This was our time for holding hands, sitting close, and listening to each other. We would eat popcorn, watch television, talk, smile, and laugh. With all the anxiety of living in a drafty house, having more month than money, and our hectic schedules, we needed this time together to remind us that everything was manageable when we remembered we were in this together. This time also helped us develop a bond of trust and support for each other. We were building our future by spending quality time weekly together. These date nights continued as Willie moved from a singing career to a speaking career, and we gladly continue them today.

I now know why "dating your spouse" is so critical to the success of your marriage. It builds a lasting love and friendship that lives beyond the raising of your children and all the unexpected experiences of life. Time together to share the experiences you each have while apart from each other allows you to share your worlds. These must include your struggles, your successes, and your lessons learned. Your spouse needs to hear your vantage point.

I could never understand why Willie would call me "just to talk." Usually, he was in an airport or had arrived at his destination for a speech. My answers were usually short, and I'm sure I sounded annoyed that I was being pulled away from the details of running the business to chat with him.

Today, as Willie's constant traveling companion, I fully understand the reason why he would call just to talk. Constant travel is lonely and full of frustrating situations: flight delays and gate changes; figuring out how to get a rental car or other transportation from the airport to your destination; and closed restaurants by the time you arrive at your hotel. I now regret how short I was with Willie when he called just to talk. I've lived the situation and now understand it. Plus, Willie loves to talk to people and who better for him to talk to than his wife? Today, traveling together is like being on a constant date with the man I love.

Several studies in the last few years have looked at whether a date night improves the quality and stability of a relationship. The Date Night Opportunity report produced by The National Marriage Project (which has been around since 1997, and is currently housed within The University of Virginia) lists the many benefits of a dedicated date night. Here are a few they found (based on surveys of couples):

1. Date nights relieve stress by allowing couples to enjoy time with one another apart from the pressing concerns of their ordinary life.
2. Date nights help sustain the romance in the relationship.
3. Date nights cultivate a sense of together-ness—an "us" mentality rather than me or you.

4. Date nights encourage couples to talk and share their feelings, which deepens their understanding of one another.

We encourage you to implement dedicated date nights in your schedules. The time set aside will give you space to work on building emotional, loving, tender connections that bind you to each other. We can attest that it works.

As we close this chapter about taking the time to constantly work on your relationship, we want to share a song that we both love. It is by our friend John Stoddart, who is one of the brightest jazz gospel musicians in the world. He is best known for his song "Angel," but there is another song he sent to us that is awesome. It speaks about the love between him and his wife, Helen, after years together and two children.

You Are!
If I could tell the story from beginning to the end
The story of a woman, believing in a man
The promise of a lifetime, still unshared
And the dream I am living now still in my head

There was you, you were there, came the answer to the prayers
So if you're wondering you're the woman for me
And if you're everything I dreamed you would be
Even after all this time I still believe
You are the one—you are

Long before the beautiful children that you gave
I was still learning what it meant to be brave

There was you—you were there
You're the answer to my prayer
If you're wondering you're the woman for me
And if you're everything I dreamed you would be
Even after all this time I still believe
You are the one you are

You are
Wonderful—incredible
From the inside out you're beautiful
You're everything I dreamed you would be
Even after all this time I still believe
You are the one

And if God let me choose the girl of my dreams
You are the one. You are!

♥ JOLLEY ADVICE

1. **Commit to dating your spouse.** It's absolutely essential to the health of your marriage.
2. **Study your spouse.** Identify what turns them on, and share what you want as well. Then give them what they want in fresh and new ways.
3. **Set a weekly date night** in your calendar, and make it a priority.
4. **Tell your spouse you love them every day.**
5. **Hold hands,** because that is how you hold each other's hearts.

♥

CHAPTER TEN

Count the Costs: Money Matters!

*"Many couples are so busy being romantic that they forget
to talk about anything practical, like personal finances.
Money management is not a romantic subject,
but marriage should be seen as entering into
a financial as well as a romantic partnership."*
~ *Financial Planner Sheryl Garrett*

WILLIE'S PERSPECTIVE

Money is considered to be one of the three main reasons that marriages break up, along with sex and communication. We have found that marriage is not just a love relationship, but also a business relationship. No matter how much you love someone, or how much fun you have together, you must pay for that fun at some point. You must pay for housing, food, transportation, and health care. And if there are children involved, you will have additional costs, including childcare, clothing, doctors bills, and a quality education. According to a report released by the Department of Agriculture in 2017, a middle-income, married couple with two children is estimated to spend $233,610 to raise a child born in 2015. Worse yet, that only covers costs from birth through age seventeen—with no mention of the costs of private school or college education expenses!

You've probably heard these sayings "It really is about the money, honey" and "There can be no romance, without finance." Well, this is true. We've counseled many couples with money problems, and we've learned that not having enough monthly income can strain any relationship. But most of the time, the bigger problem in marriage is not the amount of money being earned, but how the money is being managed. The great news we are happy to share is - money management is something you can learn!

ONE BIG MONEY POT VERSUS MULTIPLE POTS

After interviewing a number of happily married couples to see how they handled money, we identified three major approaches to money management: With the "one-pot" approach, all the money the couple earns goes into one account, and one person manages the finances with input from the other. With the "two-pot" approach, the monthly bills are split between the two people. For instance, one person handles the rent and the other handles the utilities, and so forth. The third option is the "three or more pots" approach. This is where a monthly budget is established and the spouses each contribute to a joint household account to take care of the monthly bills. One person typically oversees that account and writes the checks, with the counsel and participation of the other spouse. In our research and interviews we have found that the "age and stage" of the couple tends to determine the approach that is used.

Age and Stage Influence

The one-pot approach is typically chosen by people who get married right out of high school or college. They are usually at the start of their careers, with no assets and very little money, but willing to work together to achieve the life of their dreams. Our dear friends Kenny Glass (an executive with General Motors) and his wife of over forty years, Rudene, use this approach. When they married, their only asset was love. They were both young and right out of college. They happily lived off Kenny's salary and found that Rudene was a good money manager, so she handled the checkbook. They had three children, and Rudene stayed at home to focus on raising them while Kenny climbed the corporate ladder. When the last child started school, Rudene started working. The money she earned was banked and provided the extra financial cushion for the family. After all the children had left the nest, they stayed with the one-pot approach because it works for them.

With the two-pot approach each spouse has an income and the bills are split between the two of them. Such as, one takes the utility bills and the other takes the mortgage. Our friends Ronny and Olenthia (Len) Boardley use this method. If they have a bill that is larger than expected or an entirely unexpected bill, they sit down to reconfigure the payments on an as-needed basis. Ronny said both of them came from households that used this approach, and they decided to do the same when they got married.

People who marry later in life tend to use the three-pot approach. Usually, these people have built their careers and managed their own housing before meeting their spouse. Most often, these adults have grown accustomed to making all of the money decisions on their own. In these situations, children, property, and substantial investments also came with the marriage. Maintaining the account that they came to the marriage with, as well as joint bank accounts, is a common occurrence. This is how it works: Each person has the account that they came to the marriage with. They then add each other's name to those accounts (in case of emergencies or illness). Then they create a joint household account that each person contributes to and from which the monthly bills are paid. A monthly budget is created for this account, and they jointly discuss the bills and write the household expenses from that account.

When I interviewed Washington Post syndicated financial columnist and best-selling financial author Michelle Singletary about her thoughts on the financial approach to marriage, she shared a number of ideas. No matter what approach you choose, she said, you must talk about the money. She said that communication is the key to the success or failure of any money management plan. Michelle and her husband prefer the one-pot approach. She was not excited about the two-pot approach because she found that to be akin to having a roommate rather than a spouse. She said this about the two-pot approach: "A marriage without shared goals and shared money is just a joint venture." She could understand why the three-pot approach works well for some couples, but stressed that all accounts should have both spouse's names on them, and she was adamant that there should be no secret or hidden accounts between couples. Michelle believes this arrangement can sow seeds of distrust in a marriage. She noted it does not create Godly unity in the marriage, and it takes unity to win together.

Teamwork Makes the Dream Work

No matter which approach fits your family, the most important ingredient is that you talk to each other and be open and honest about your finances. The bottom line is that financial accounts can be complicated, and must be discussed and reviewed in great detail. Then you decide the plan that works best for both of you, and work your plan.

Our friends Ron and Gladys Pemberton use the three-pot approach and shared how they had to make major adjustments when they first got married. They started by setting short-term and long-range goals to achieve what they wanted to accomplish, and a budget that they would use to accomplish those goals.

Ron says that a critical component of their success, after setting the budget, was to go from a "Me, Me, Me" mindset to a "We, We, We" mindset. He confessed that it took him a while to figure this out. A major mistake in the first few years of their marriage helped him realize the importance of a "We" mindset.

Ron liked nice cars and when he was single, he typically bought a new one every year. One day, he saw a beautiful new Mercedes as he rode by a dealership and stopped in to talk to a salesman. He said to himself, "This would be great for me and Gladys to ride around in." So, he bought the car! When he got home, he showed Gladys the new car, but she was not happy.

They had a baby on the way and he had not talked to her about buying the car. She reminded him that they were a team, and even though they used the three-pot approach to managing their money, their decisions were to be made as a "Team of We." He said that was the first and last time he made a major financial decision without talking to his wife. The most important lesson here is the value of communication and collaboration. Remember, it takes teamwork to make a dream work.

Stephen and Andi Bullock also shared a compelling story about teamwork. He was divorced and she had never been married. Both were successful professionals. When they married, they also established the three-pot approach to their marriage's financial management.

Stephen is an attorney and had his own firm. Sometime after they got married, he had a big case and it took all of his time and resources. While waiting for the case to settle, he personally funded his business from savings. The deal took much longer than he anticipated to close, and he ended up with an empty bank account. Reluctantly, he told Andi and she said, "Don't worry, I've got you. We're in this together." The deal eventually came through, and the first check he wrote was a big check to his wife. The money not only repaid her financial investment in him, but also thanked her for her faith in him. Stephen emphasized the power of working as a team when it comes to your financial matters.

When Dee and I got married, we discussed our prior life experiences, how we managed our finances, and our personal preferences as it related to money management. We also came to the conclusion that the three-pot approach to money management would work best for us. Dee had lived alone and managed her own affairs for years before I entered her life. In fact, when she returned to her hometown of Hampton, Virginia, she became the administrator for her father's church. She was so adept at money management that she coordinated the construction-bond project that helped raise half a million dollars for the renovation of their church's sanctuary. I, on the other hand, had always lived at home and was well known for being very frugal with every dollar. In other words, I was notoriously cheap!

The one-pot concept would not have been a good idea for us. Dee did not want to ask me if she could buy a pair of shoes or personal items, and I did not want to be concerned, or have an issue if she bought a pair of shoes, especially if they were bought with "household" money. Instead, Dee and I decided she would keep the personal account she had before we were married and I would keep mine. We added our names to each other's accounts and discussed all our financial obligations.

Next, we worked out our Jolley household budget and decided (based on our individual incomes) what we each should contribute to the joint Jolley household account. Since Dee was great with financial details, we decided she would write the checks and balance the accounts. To this day, we sit together to review our monthly household expenses and what is to be paid. Any non-budgeted items that may come out of that household account are discussed and agreed upon before a purchase is made. Once we make our contributions to the household account and all the bills are paid, we become good to go with our personal purchases. We have successfully operated within this system for over thirty years, and we have never had a disagreement about finances. She can buy fashionable shoes, and I can buy my technology toys, and neither of us has to worry about the other's spending. Hallelujah!

DEE'S PERSPECTIVE

It was a bright spring day when Willie came to me with a big smile. "I'm ready for the tax man!" he proclaimed. He placed a wrinkled brown grocery bag on the corner of my desk. "What's that for?" I asked. "Those are my receipts and bank statements for the year. All ready for the tax preparer." I was speechless.

This was our first personal tax return preparation as a couple. Since I had worked the administrative side of Mom and Dad's businesses, including their church, I understood financial details. That made it easy for us to agree that I should be responsible for getting the taxes done. At the time, we were getting ready to visit a local tax preparer, and I assumed this would be a breeze.

But assumptions are never good, especially when it comes to couples and anything money related. I made the mistake of assuming that Willie would have his summary list of personal expenses. These included items like medical and dental bills, donations to our home church, and any out-of-pocket business expenditures that we may have overlooked previously. Naturally, I thought that his information would look like mine—listed on a sheet of paper with the supportive information attached. Instead, there sat this wrinkled brown grocery bag on the corner of my desk, filled with receipts with little notes on them. That was Willie's tax filing system! He seemed so proud that he had all his little receipts together, but my organized mind was traumatized. Talk about a hot mess! Fortunately, I realized this was not the time for me to communicate that and hurt his feelings, because he was so proud to be prepared for completing our taxes.

In the years preceding this special moment with Willie and his wrinkled brown paper bag, I had helped run my parents' businesses, including their grocery store, laundry mat, hair salon, and barber shop. I also served as church administrator, managing many of the daily operations. We had systems, reports, and checks and balances. Organization was second nature for me, and I thought everyone else functioned the same way. I was wrong.

I'd married a singer who was often paid in cash, and the brown paper bag made me realize his "accounting system" was more like flying by the seat of his pants. After I recovered from the shock of it all, I realized we needed to have a frank, yet friendly discussion about our financial procedures. I sought to give him a different perspective on how to organize and prepare for financial reporting. Willie and I sat down to talk, and I recommended we use some of the financial practices and forms we used to run my parent's businesses and modify them to fit our needs.

As a solo businessman, Willie had built his business from the ground up. He was used to making all his own decisions. Yet Willie said, "Okay, I trust you. Let's do it your way." Willie said that we were a team, and he was willing to learn new practices in order to better accomplish our goals.

From that experience, we developed not only a financial accounting system, but a system for handling difficult decisions—the "Four F's" for handling tough conversations. The Four F's are to be friendly, frank, fair, and focused on a positive result. Let's look at each.

- **Friendly.** In your marriage, there will be many times when you will want to say what I was thinking when I saw Willie's wrinkled brown paper bag: this is a hot mess! Instead, you must handle those difficult conversations and negotiations with grace and mutual respect to achieve the desired outcome. Whether the conversations are about finances, child rearing, job decisions, or something else, it will be necessary to talk it out until you reach a result you both can live with and support. These discussions require staying friendly with your tone and your demeanor. Arguing and mean-spiritedness will only create unnecessary issues that expand the problems and take you off message and off focus. Stay friendly in your delivery.
- **Frank.** Being frank about the situation is not a license to be rude. Rather, you can calmly tell the truth and share the facts. A problem cannot be solved if it is hidden or masked. Be frank, but with respect, and share all the facts about the situation, so it can be fixed.
- **Fair.** If both parties go into a tough discussion with the mindset that they are committed to being just and

balanced in their dealings with each other, the conversation usually goes better and generates less stress. Practice listening without prejudging and coming into the conversation with a willingness to consider your spouse's point of view. Willie and I exhibit this by trusting each other and avoiding the trap of thinking our individual way is the only way.

- **Focused on a positive result.** Successful couples work together and share the power because they always want to end up with a positive result. When you make a commitment to stay focused on a positive result, you will not become distracted by minor issues.

One major test of the Four F's came when we purchased our first contact management system for the business. I had been working with Willie for a few months. Money was tight, but he was getting more speaking engagements and creating some financial breathing space. We needed a database to keep up with the contacts we were developing, and I'd heard about a new database program. Since we didn't know much about contact management systems, I talked Willie into the idea of a consultant who would help install the system and input the contacts. Her hourly rate was $250, and I expected it to take about three hours. Willie reminded me of our tight finances and was reluctant to even pay for three hours. At that point in his career, $750 took quite a while to generate. Nevertheless, he gave in to my desire to upgrade our technology because I was confident it would take less than three hours to get the work done. I was quite mistaken. She ended up taking over eight hours and costing over two thousand dollars!

When the consultant presented us with the final bill that evening, Willie was speechless. I could see the steam coming out of his ears! He excused himself, saying he needed to go out. He left the office and went for a drive to calm down.

I paid the consultant but felt terrible. I was over budget and Willie was rightfully upset. He had trusted me to do the due diligence for this project, and I had failed. Worse, he hadn't wanted to spend any money in the first place! When he returned, we discussed what had happened that evening, and how we could prevent a similar scenario from happening again. More due diligence? Asking for several proposals? Negotiating an all-inclusive price? We were calm and respectful of each other, although we were sad about the financial setback we had that day. But we worked through it, because he confirmed we were in it together.

You are going to have some financial setbacks in life, and as married couples you must be willing to work through them so your marriage will not just survive but thrive. Interestingly enough, we went through this experience years before Willie wrote the book *A Setback Is A Setup For A Comeback*. But I believe the principles he teaches in that book were established during the earlier challenging experiences we had as a couple. If you have not read that book, I recommend you read it. It will help you grow your thinking and your willingness to keep working through your financial setbacks, so you not only survive them, but thrive as a result of them.

❤ JOLLEY ADVICE

1. **Get on the same page** by first discussing how each of you view money, debt, saving, investing, retirement, and financial freedom.
2. **Each of you should prepare your list of financial liabilities and assets so you know where you are individually.** Share these lists with each other. When you marry, you marry your spouse's financial life.

If either of you has any money problems, develop a plan to straighten them out, then execute it.

3. **Discuss your mutual financial goals (short-term and long-term) for your marriage (household and family).** Then set about building your plan for one year, five years, ten years, twenty years to reach them. Take the example of a ship's captain preparing for a trip at sea. Chart your course to your ideal destination now, and be prepared to reconfigure later. A ship without an initial course of destination will be lost at sea.

4. **Decide on your approach to household money management.** Will you use the one-pot, two-pot, or three-pot approach?

5. **Use the Four F's—friendly, frank, fair, and focused** on a positive result—when engaging in difficult discussions.

6. **Take classes together and attend financial planning workshops to help you become familiar with the terminology and approaches to financial planning.** Then interview several financial advisors and select one (or more than one) that can help you meet your goals.

7. **Plan your investment accounts for retirement or late-life enhancement.** These include brokerage accounts, 401Ks, ROTHs, real estate holdings, and other income streams. The more you do this, the easier it becomes for both of you to learn to read your financial story.

8. **Write your wills and talk about spousal survivorship.**
   A Charles Schwab Center for Financial Research study
   shows that while women live longer than men, their out
   of pocket medical expenses are higher by as much as 24
   percent. Therefore, it is imperative to plan ahead.
9. **Make sure there is enough life insurance to replace
   the income of the person who passes away.**
10. **Become familiar with your Social Security pension
    and the rights and limits that come along with it.**

For Those Not Yet Married

♥

For Those Not Yet Married

"A happy marriage is like a long conversation
which always seems too short."
~ *Andre Maurois*

MAKE A "THOUGHT-FULL" DECISION

Life involves many major decisions, but the most important decision you will make (after the decision about your faith) is who you choose to marry. The person you marry will be responsible for 90 percent of your misery or 90 percent of your joy! That person will impact every aspect of your life, so choose wisely. Please do not make an emotional decision. Make a "thought-full" decision. This means before you say, "I do," you should do some non-emotional thinking. That way you can make a decision in a clear and analytical manner. As our pastor, John K. Jenkins Sr., says, "Brothers, you must go beyond the butt and the breasts and get to the brains and beliefs. And sisters, you must get past the 'fine' and 'find' a person of character."

We believe that God has set out principles about finding a good spouse, and scripture gives us great direction. We also believe that you must make a point to learn about the person you are planning to marry and get to know them well before getting married. Spend time, a lot of time, talking. Learn about your potential spouse's values, virtues, and perspectives on life. Take time to see if this is really a friendship or if it's a passing infatuation.

Also, we believe you must seek direction from God. Scripture states, ""House and land are handed down from parents, but a congenial spouse comes straight from God." Proverbs 19:14 (MSG)

With this in mind, we recommend you pray and ask for clarity when choosing a spouse. I know I did. I prayed and God gave me a clear answer that Dee was the one for me. She ironed my shirt! That's right: she ironed my shirt. It may sound strange, but that was the factor that made it clear for me.

I had been dating another woman before I met Dee, and one day when I was running late for an event, she stopped by my house. I needed help to get out of the door so I wouldn't be late, and I asked her to iron my shirt while I got my items together for the event. She looked at me like I had lost my mind and said, "No. You iron it yourself!" I made a mental note right then that this lady may be beautiful, but she may not be the one. She was nice, but I was not sure that she would be a good partner for me in working together to build a life and a business. I also asked God to please give me clarity about whether this was a big deal or just a small bump in the road. In time, I got clarity and that relationship ended.

Later, after a few other relationships, I met Dee. One weekend I went to Hampton, Virginia, with her to visit her parents. We were preparing to go to church on a Sunday morning and were running a little behind after enjoying her mom's delicious breakfast. As I was getting my clothes together, Dee came and took my dress shirt and said, "You go ahead

and get your shower and I will take care of ironing your shirt."
What? I had not asked her, but she saw my need and took
action. It was confirmation to me that she would be a good
partner in life and business. Thirty years later I continue to
see that simple gesture as a good sign, and I know I made a
good choice. Always ask God for clarity on who you should
marry; God will find a way to show you—even if it's with an
iron and a wrinkly shirt.

We have found that scripture gives us direction on how
to make a wise choice. Here are four verses to consider and
meditate on:

- Jeremiah 29:11 says, "For I know the plans I have
  for you, declares the Lord. Plans of peace and not
  of evil, to give you a future and a hope. Call on Me
  and pray to Me and I will listen to you!" (In other
  words, pray before you say "I do"!)
- Proverbs 18:22 says, "He who finds a wife, finds a
  good thing, and obtains favor from the Lord." (Be
  diligent in your search and you will find a good thing
  and will obtain favor.)
- Ecclesiastes 4:9 says, "Two are better than one,
  because they have good reward for their work
  together." (It takes work and time, but it is worth
  the effort as two of you together is stronger than
  one all alone.)
- Matthew 19: 5–6 says, "For this reason, a man shall
  leave his father and mother and be joined to his wife,
  and the two shall become one flesh. Therefore, what
  God has joined together, let no man separate."

In the marriage vows there is a statement that says, "What God has put together let no man put asunder!" My friend, Bishop AJ Wright, says, some people think God put them together, when in reality, circumstances put them together. That is why you must pray and seek God to determine who you should marry. According to Bishop Wright, people who marry for circumstances often marry the wrong person, and then they want God to fix it! The circumstances might be getting married to get a green card, getting married because their biological clock is ticking, or getting married because all of their friends are getting married. They need somebody, anybody! Their circumstances make the critical marriage decision for them. But using circumstances to determine your life partner can lead to a lousy life.

While teaching a class for the American Management Association (AMA), Dee met a corporate executive who was impressed with how she spoke so glowingly about her husband and her marriage. He was intrigued, and asked Dee to introduce him to me. He wanted to see if my thoughts about the marriage were the same as hers. He wanted a man's perspective.

I met him for lunch and shared my views, which he said mirrored Dee's. He called Dee later and said he was impressed, and asked if he could take us both to dinner. We agreed and assumed we would meet his wife at dinner as well. As we left home for the dinner, Dee and I discussed what we might talk to the couple about. Maybe we would just chat about our careers and the challenges of raising children. Maybe he and his wife were trying to improve their relationship, and wanted to know what was working for us. Or maybe they were having serious challenges, and we would do marriage triage to try and fix it. We were open to whatever topic they wanted to discuss and looked forward to a friendly dinner of getting to know this couple.

When we got to the restaurant, he was alone. As it turned out, he and his wife were separated and living in different homes. They rarely spoke. He said he was in a miserable marriage and just wanted to meet people who could give him hope that a happy marriage was possible! He told us that his parents divorced when he was young. He adored his parents, but seldom got to see what he thought was a loving husband and wife relationship.

When he graduated from college and started his climb up the corporate ladder, a business associate told him that if he was serious about quickly getting to the top in his company, he needed to have a wife who was cultured, attractive, and could help him navigate the corporate game to the C-suite. He found and married a woman who had all of the attributes he needed. She could be the perfect corporate wife, but beyond that, they had nothing in common. They were not friends. They had completely different values and really didn't even enjoy each other's company. He quickly rose up the corporate ladder, but paid a heavy price in the process. While he had achieved his career goals, his personal life was in shambles. He had married the wrong person for the wrong reasons.

In addition to meeting people who marry for status, Dee and I often meet people who marry only because of sex. They enjoy the sex, but there is nothing else going on with their relationship. They get married and hope the sex alone will sustain the marriage. Unfortunately, many of these couples end up divorced.

Don't worry—I am not saying that you should marry someone only for friendship. Physical attraction is important as well. In fact, physical attraction is most often where relationships begin. It's human nature to be attracted to a person with your eyes. Yet, once you are attracted physically, you cannot settle just for that. You must continue to work on the relationship because great relationships involve being together outside the bedroom as well as in the bedroom. This involves making sure you enjoy and respect each other, and that starts by making sure you truly enjoy each other's company and are really friends.

I can tell you, I was first attracted to my wife the day I saw her walking down the street, and I'm still attracted to her. She still turns me on! Yet we are great friends. In fact, she is my best friend.

THE FIVE-DAY TEST

In order to test your friendship, I recommend you try my five-day test. Go on a five-day trip together in which you don't engage in any sexual activity. You need these five sex free days because sex clouds the mind: it can make you do crazy things, think crazy thoughts, and keep you from seeing clearly. Spend five dedicated days together. The key is that you spend lots of time in each other's presence and really get to know each other.

During these five days, discuss your views and values. Talk about hurts, habits, and hang-ups, and see how open and honest you can be with each other. It is amazing how relationships can be established or revealed through open and honest conversations. Dee and I did this. We had a retreat in Harper's Ferry, West Virginia. She was deciding if she could trust me and quizzed me endlessly about my musician's life and how theology and music fit together. I wanted to know the details of her first marriage and why it didn't work.

THE THIRTY-DAY TEST

If you're in a long-distance relationship, it's critical to spend at least thirty days in the same city before you decide to get married. I have dear friends who dated long distance for all their college years. When they graduated, they got jobs in different cities. They would get together for weekends once or twice a month and go out to dinner on Friday, then to a movie or a theatrical play on Saturday night. They'd share Sunday brunch and then go back to their respective cities. It was a fantasy island type of weekend every time they were together. Perfect! No jobs, no cooking, no cleaning of the house—just perfect little weekend vacations.

But real life is not like that! They never lived in the same city for thirty days, and they got married about six months after graduating from college. Once married, they moved to the same city and lived together for the first time ever. Their perfect, fairy-tale vision of marriage was not what they received when they had to live together for an extended period of time. Their marriage lasted about a year. They separated and divorced the following year.

This couple had an unrealistic view of each other because they had not spent time getting to know each other. Their marriage was doomed to fail. So for those who are serious and thinking about marriage, we recommend that you look at your future together realistically and choose wisely.

SEEK WISE COUNSEL FROM PEOPLE WHO ARE HAPPILY MARRIED

When Dee and I were dating, we sought counsel from people who were happily married, and we continued to do so after we were married. Over the years, we have gotten incredibly valuable advice from people who have been married twenty, thirty, forty, fifty, and even sixty years. Two of those people are Kenneth and Bernice Mitchell. When we interviewed them, they had been married for over sixty years and were still going strong. Here is some counsel they shared that can be helpful for those considering marriage as well as for those who are already married:

1. Take time to know the person you are thinking about marrying very well before you say I do. Take your time to really learn about them so you can find out if they are the real person or a representative of that person.
2. It is important to have role models you can talk to about your marriage. They can help you work through the problems. And never, ever obtain marriage advice from people who are not happily married!
3. You must not go to bed mad. It only causes the issue to fester and become worse. Kiss, make up, and move on!
4. Keep having fun! Marriage is a skill and it takes work, but it is also wonderful and fun. So keep the fun while continuing to do the work. It is worth it!

ZIG ZIGLAR'S QUOTE ON MARRIAGE

"I have no way of knowing whether or not you married the wrong person, but I do know that many people have a lot of wrong ideas about marriage and what it takes to make that marriage happy and successful.

I'll be the first to admit that it's possible that you did marry the wrong person. However, if you treat the wrong person like the right person, you could well end up having married the right person after all.

On the other hand, if you marry the right person, and treat that person wrong, you certainly will have ended up marrying the wrong person. I also know that it is far more important to be the right kind of person than it is to marry the right person. In short, whether you married the right or wrong person is primarily up to you."

The Little Things

We hope you are blessed by this book and that your marriage will be strengthened as a result of it. We have learned that when all is said and done, much more is said than actually done. A good marriage requires more than the right words; it requires doing the right things (which are often small things) over and over again,

If your feelings are hurt, tell your spouse and don't hold it in. If you hurt your spouse's feelings, apologize quickly, so you can move on. Take care of the little things, and there will be fewer and fewer big things to deal with. Remember: small issues become bigger issues if they are not dealt with when they're small and manageable.

We leave you with the lyrics of a song that my brother, Noble, wrote for his wedding day. I recorded the song, and it is part of the collection of songs on our marriage enrichment CD. We know that people struggle with relationships and many couples struggle with the process of creating a happy and fulfilling marriage. So, this book is just the first of many that we have in store for helping people have happy and fulfilling relationships.

In the future you can look for materials and programs from us on how to have a successful blended family, how to have successful marriages where the spouses work together, and how to raise successful children, even when they don't want to cooperate.

Thank you for investing your time to read this book. We believe that the investment will pay great dividends in your marriage and in your family. Remember it is all about the Little Things! God bless you!

Little Things
by Noble Jolley, Sr.
Performed by Dr. Willie Jolley

Little things that don't seem big—they really mean a lot
to me
Those little things that make me smile my love
Those little things that you do, that make me glad
there's me and you
Now you've made my life a paradise of joy
It's the little things—that mean so much to me
The way you smile- the way you look at me
Like a child- I'm happy as can be with you
Little things that you say paint pictures in my mind each day
Of what you think and how you really feel
We're past the point of playing games, we know
each other's little ways
Now it's open road for the love we share
It's the little things- that mean so much to me
The way you smile—the way you look at me
Like a child—I'm happy as can be with you, you ....
It's the little things that make my life complete
Your tender touch, the sweet words that you speak

Say so much, even if it's just—hello
It's the little things—that mean so much to me
The way you smile—the way you look at me
Like a child—I'm happy as can be with you

It's the little things that make my life complete
Your tender touch, the sweet words that you speak
Say so much, even if it's just—hello,
Hello! I love the little things you do

Final Thoughts by Willie & Dee Jolley

We thank you for reading this book! This has truly been a labor of love. We wrote in a spirit of love for each other, but also because we love you! We love people, and wanted to help more people to have better relationships, and more couples to experience the love and joy we experience in our marriage.

Our goal was to write a relationship book that was captivating, compelling and life changing. We believed our message would positively impact couples. We felt that if we positively impacted couples, they in turn would positively impact their families and friends; and each family member and friend would positively impact their communities; and those communities would positively impact the world!

So, if you are reading this page, that probably means you have completed the book. You are a rare one! Most people buy books and read a few pages and then set them on a shelf where they collect dust. We have learned that success in any venture must be a matter of "Self- Help" and not "Shelf-Help!"

Now that you have read the book, it is time to do the work necessary to shape your great marriage. Just as a potter shapes clay into a masterpiece, you must do the work to shape your marriage into a masterpiece.

You both should go through the Jolley Advice sections. Discuss any notes, insights and ideas! Are you close in your thinking?

How can you get closer? We also recommend that you go to our website (WillieJolley.com/3m) and purchase the companion workbook. Complete the exercises and action steps and you will start to see your marriage improve.

Our Hopes!

We hope this book has been a blessing to you and your spouse. As a result, we hope you will be a blessing to others in your circle and share your new insights with them.

We hope you will let us know how you are doing. Send us an email or video message to info@williejolley.com letting us know the impact this book has had on you and your marriage.

We hope that you will post positive reviews and testimonials on Amazon.com and other online portals.

We hope you will stay connected to us by signing up to our newsletter (WillieJolley.com/gift) and on all social media platforms. We will update you on what we are doing new that could be a blessing to you and your family.

We hope to personally meet you at our events.

We hope you will get copies of this book and give them as gifts to people you love.

Most importantly, we hope you will give God the Glory for this book! We believe this book didn't come "from us" as it came "through us!" And we want to encourage you to do what we do, connect on a personal level with God.

Throughout this book, we have shared that next to your faith, who you marry will be your most important decision. This means that we believe the most important decision you will ever make is your decision to trust God! If you want more information on this, visit JolleyGoodNews.org and hit the "Faith Forward" tab!

May God bless you and keep you...and we pray that you have great success in your marriage. Keep the faith and remember, we believe in you and believe your best is yet to come! Amen!